CW00923134

Kitty Fisher

Kitty Fisher

The First Female Celebrity

Joanne Major

PEN & SWORD HISTORY

First published in Great Britain in 2022 by
Pen & Sword History
An imprint of
Pen & Sword Books Ltd
Yorkshire – Philadelphia

ISBN 978 1 39900 697 2

Typeset by Mac Style
Printed and bound in the UK by CPI Group (UK) Ltd,
Croydon, CR0 4YY.

Pen & Sword Books Limited incorporates the imprints of Atlas,
Archaeology, Aviation, Discovery, Family History, Fiction, History,
Maritime, Military, Military Classics, Politics, Select, Transport,
True Crime, Air World, Frontline Publishing, Leo Cooper, Remember
When, Seaforth Publishing, The Praetorian Press, Wharncliffe
Local History, Wharncliffe Transport, Wharncliffe True Crime
and White Owl.

For a complete list of Pen & Sword titles please contact

PEN & SWORD BOOKS LIMITED
47 Church Street, Barnsley, South Yorkshire, S70 2AS, England
E-mail: enquiries@pen-and-sword.co.uk
Website: www.pen-and-sword.co.uk

Or

PEN AND SWORD BOOKS
1950 Lawrence Rd, Havertown, PA 19083, USA
E-mail: Uspen-and-sword@casematepublishers.com
Website: www.penandswordbooks.com

For Oakley

Contents

Acknowledgements

When I started to research Kitty Fisher's life, I had planned research trips to various areas of the country to consult archives, to view portraits, or to walk in Kitty's footsteps. Then the pandemic hit and suddenly nothing was quite so simple. I would, therefore, like to thank the staff at numerous record offices, libraries, and art galleries who have supplied information remotely. In particular, special mention must go to the people whom I have pestered at the National Library of Scotland, Goldsmiths Library, Canterbury Museums and Galleries, Staffordshire Archives, and Kent Archives. Please know that I appreciate the time and trouble you have taken to answer my queries and – in several cases – to go above and beyond in your assistance.

I would also like to thank the staff on the Creative Writing degree programme at the University of Lincoln, Dr Christopher Dows, Dr Sarah Stovell, Dr Sue Healy, Dr Daniele Pantano, Dr Guy Mankowski, and Dr Amy Lilwall. Their advice, guidance, and excellent teaching have been invaluable. I am looking forward to beginning a Creative Writing MA with the University of Lincoln in 2022.

My thanks go to Sir William and Lady Proby for allowing me to reproduce their portrait of Kitty Fisher by Sir Joshua Reynolds, and to the staff of the Elton Estate Office. Also to Guy Innes and Alexandra Sheldon at Titsey Hall, who shared with me a great deal of information.

For their assistance in either answering my questions or digitising images (and sometimes for both!), I must also especially thank the relevant staff at the National Portrait Gallery, the Yale Center for British Art, the Lewis Walpole Library, and the Harvard Art Museums. My thanks also go to the other institutions who have made available their portraits and prints.

My publisher, Pen and Sword, has been, as always, amazing. Particular thanks go to Jonathan Wright and also to Charlotte Mitchell for her help and patience in dealing with my queries and emails. Also to my copy editor, Cecily Blench.

Lastly, I must mention my family for their support and encouragement whilst I lost myself in research and writing. My love and thanks go to my husband, Sam, my children, Luke and Aeron, and their partners, Chelsea and Sam. I couldn't have done this without you.

Introduction

'All that we can know of her
Is this... she was a milliner.
Her parentage so low and mean
Is hardly to be trac'd, I ween:
Say, has she wit... or has she sense?
No! nothing but impertinence.'

(*Kitty's Stream*, 1759)

The eighteenth-century author who scribbled down these lines at the height of Catherine Maria Fischer's fame was off the mark with his description. The vivacious Kitty Fisher, as Catherine Maria became known, was never impertinent except, perhaps, to her society's strict rules that governed – and censured – a woman's conduct. As for wit, sense, and good humour, Kitty had those qualities in abundance. Added to which, she was kind-hearted and – despite her profession as a courtesan – possessed of innate elegance and modesty. Petite, with rich chestnut hair, cerulean blue eyes, and a *retroussé* (upturned) nose, Kitty was pretty rather than an exceptional beauty. It was her personality coupled with her looks that made her irresistible. Men wanted Kitty and women wanted to look like her. The incomparable Kitty Fisher was the eighteenth-century version of an 'it girl'.

Catapulted into the public gaze after a horse-riding accident, Kitty's world changed overnight. Before long, her name – or rather, the pseudonym by which she became known – would travel around the globe. It was a long way from her humble beginnings. Kitty's family were working-class; her father was a London tradesman.

Mr Fischer's one great fault was that he idolised Kitty, his eldest child, to the point of ruin and the detriment of his business. He taught her to expect more than her parents' frugal lifestyle. In doing so, Kitty's father innocently set in motion a chain of events that led his daughter into a life of infamy. While still a teenager, Kitty became – for a short but exhilarating period – one of London's most dazzling, iconic celebrities. She was a 'celebrated courtesan', a kept mistress who was adored and decried in equal measure. In contrast to her contemporaries, those other infamous 'ladies of the town', it is Kitty's name that has echoed through the centuries. Incongruously, her notoriety survives in part via a children's nursery rhyme: 'Lucy Locket lost her pocket, / Kitty Fisher found it, / not a penny was there in it, / only ribbon round it.' For someone whose name is so well known today, little is remembered of her other than the scandal of her life, myths, and half-truths. It comes as something of a surprise to learn that Kitty's career in the capital's upmarket sex trade was brief and that there is so much more of her story to tell. Like her father before her, Kitty had one crucial flaw, one that proved a big obstacle for someone in her profession. Kitty fell in love far too easily.

The purpose of this book is not to compare and contrast eighteenth-century attitudes to women – in particular, those who earned their living in the sex industry – with today's society. Kitty was a woman very much of her time, as were the men who paid her bills and bought her jewels. It was a licentious, lascivious era. If a 'woman of the town' received a complimentary write-up in *Harris's List of Covent-Garden Ladies* (or *A Man of Pleasure's Kalendar*), the gentleman's handbook of the capital's whores, she viewed it as a success. Inclusion within the pages of *Harris's List* could lead to a position in one of the city's better brothels, or even the chance to be 'taken into keeping'. Kitty never viewed herself as a common prostitute: she was a courtesan. Her ultimate aim was a marriage to a wealthy man and all the security which that would bring with it. If she gained a title into the bargain, then all well and good. While it was no small task, it was not out of reach. Before Kitty lay the examples of the well-born but penniless

Gunning sisters, Elizabeth and Maria, who toyed with appearing on the stage of Dublin's theatre. They both attracted the attention – and hands in marriage – of peers of the realm: James Hamilton, 6th Duke of Hamilton, and George William Coventry, 6th Earl of Coventry, respectively. Maria, Countess of Coventry, was Kitty's greatest rival as well as a role model. There was also the flower girl and prostitute, Fanny Murray, who married twice; her first husband was a baronet who left her little but debts when he died, but with her second husband, an actor, Fanny had a long-lasting and happy, if otherwise unremarkable, marriage. Others in Kitty's sphere did not fare so well; Nelly O'Brien was the talk of the town for a while and gave the Earl of Thanet three sons, but was dismissed from his house when he married a titled lady instead. Lucy Cooper was immortalised in verse as 'that damnation whore of hell' and neither snared a husband nor thought to save for the days when her looks began to fade and she was eclipsed by younger rivals. She ended her days in squalid penury, incarcerated in a debtors' prison. At a time when opportunities for women were limited, the sex industry offered a route to independence or marital security and sometimes, for the lucky few, to both.

However, the fleeting career of a superstar 'celebrated' courtesan was beset by perils, as Lucy Cooper found out. Due to her instant celebrity, Kitty Fisher eclipsed her rivals, only to find that a life of ignominy was not to her taste. When one starts to delve into Kitty's life, it becomes clear that not only was her time as a courtesan short-lived, she also had very little luck in finding a suitable 'keeper'. Other courtesans certainly had more success, if that success was measured by being the sole mistress of a duke, marquess or even a prince. Kitty's men were lower in rank, and always temporary. Where Kitty shone was her innate knack for self-publicity, helped by Sir Joshua Reynolds and Nathaniel Hone's outstanding portraits that immortalised this intriguing woman. Kitty Fisher had star-quality, that certain 'something'. She was propelled headfirst into a life as one of the first and foremost celebrities as we understand the concept today.[1]

How did Kitty achieve this? Let's start at the beginning…

Chapter One

Sex in the City

'On some Holiday sure you was born,
In the Month of true Taste and much Mirth;
Pale Prudery skulk'd off forlorn,
And Sprightliness danc'd at your Birth.'
(*A Sketch of the Present Times and the Time to Come,*
in an Address to Kitty Fisher, 1762)

It was a warm and sunny day at the start of a long, hot summer. King Street, in London's Soho, was bustling and vibrant. Just to the north lay Soho Square and, a little beyond that, market gardens and open, rolling countryside. A short walk southwards led to the grand mansions of Piccadilly and to the Haymarket where the roads were often impassable, blocked by farmers' carts laden with hay and straw for sale. London was spreading outwards and new buildings were springing up, encroaching into the open fields beyond. The front door of a house on the south side of narrow King Street creaked opened, and a man stepped out. He leaned back against the doorframe, blinking into the sudden bright light. His friends and neighbours saw the smile on his face and rushed over, offering congratulations. Inside the house, a newborn baby began to cry.

Catherine Maria Fischer, better known as Kitty Fisher, entered the world on the first day of June 1741. Her father was delighted with the new addition to his family. Kitty was his first child and he celebrated the news by getting rolling drunk in the local taverns. John Henry Fischer was a German immigrant to the capital and, when he didn't have a pint pot in his hand, was a hard-working man. His trade was that of a silver chaser. Using a specialised hammer and punch, John spent his days etching intricate designs onto silverware which graced the tables and sideboards of families richer than his own. Kitty's mother was a Londoner, Ann Bagnell. Nine days after her birth, Kitty was carried into St Anne's, the spacious and handsome parish church that overlooked her family's home. Festivities after the ceremony carried on into the next day when the king, George II, marked the beginning of his fifteenth year on the throne. London's church bells rang out in the morning, and cannons were fired in Hyde Park and at the Tower of London. In the evening, bonfires were lit and fireworks exploded in the sky, dazzling the onlookers. The aristocracy and foreign ambassadors crowded into the capital, eager to pay their compliments to the king and dance away the night at balls and dinner parties held to mark the occasion. Kitty's parents cradled their daughter and watched in awe, dreaming of a brilliant future for their little girl. Anything seemed possible.

After Kitty, at least four more children were born to the Fischers: a daughter named Ann who didn't survive long, another bearing the same name two years later, then Sarah Louisa and last, nine years after Kitty's birth, a son named John Henry for his father. Before Kitty's tenth birthday, the family had moved to a house on nearby Grafton Street (now the Charing Cross Road). It was an indifferent address but still a respectable one. A few years later, they relocated once again, to the adjoining Moor Street. Each move was to an address not quite so good as the last. Moor Street was a short, narrow thoroughfare that was easy to overlook. The Fischers were slipping into a downward trajectory. Mr Fischer was too focused on his pretty eldest daughter, rather than on earning a living or looking after the rest of his family.[1]

Soho has a long and rich history of cosmopolitanism and immigration, stretching to the present day. From the sixteenth century, the area became a haven for religious refugees. The Protestant Reformation (originating in modern-day Germany, and from Martin Luther's beliefs) had taken hold in mainland Europe, especially in

France, where it followed Calvinistic rather than Lutheran doctrines. French conquests along the Rhine led to many Germanic Lutherans settling in France. Meanwhile, French Calvinistic Protestants, known as Huguenots, found themselves on a theological collision course with both the Catholic Church and the French monarchy. They were accused of heresy and forced to flee their country, in fear of their lives. Huguenot émigrés settled in Protestant countries. Many came to England and, in particular, to its capital city, London. Living in tight-knit groups of family and friends, the areas in which they settled were soon recognised as centres for particular trades. Spitalfields in east London became famous for silk weaving, Wandsworth for gardening, and Soho was soon known for the silver- and goldsmiths, engravers (or chasers), and tapestry weavers who congregated there. The area stood at the West End of the burgeoning city, close to the royal court and the fashionable nobility. The Soho tradesmen depended upon these rich patrons for commissions. It's not known why Kitty's father chose to leave Germany for England. After the death of the last Stuart monarch, Queen Anne, in 1714, her Hanoverian cousin had claimed the British throne, the first of four Georges to rule in succession. Since then, there had been a marked increase in the German-speaking communities in England, particularly in London. Perhaps John Henry Fischer's family had followed in the train of the old king, George I, when he came to England for his coronation? Maybe, even, they had first settled in France but travelled to England seeking more freedom and opportunities? However he may have reached London, Kitty's father, a Lutheran, felt at home in Soho.[2]

London's migrant Germanic Lutheran congregation had a dedicated church, St-Mary-le-Savoy, also known as the Savoy Chapel. It still stands today to the south of the Strand. However, Kitty's family used St Anne's in Soho for the baptisms of their children. John Henry Fischer chose to worship in the church which stood alongside his home with his neighbours, rather than keep within his ancestral community. Kitty grew up among these neighbours in the maze of streets between Soho Square and Leicester Fields. The area was one of industry and shabby gentility, rubbing shoulders with the emergent – and more upmarket – West End of London. Hers was a close-knit community, a dynamic mix of religion, trade, and fashion. The streets buzzed with different languages and accents, a cultural hotch-potch. From the start, Kitty glimpsed a different, more exciting life, one close but just out of reach.

Alongside, however, there were also dangers. Right there, almost on the Fischer family's doorstep, was not only the capital's fashionable West End but also Covent Garden, with its attendant vices. By day, Covent Garden was a marketplace. Early in the morning, the stallholders would arrive laden with baskets of vegetables, fruit, and flowers. While they set up for the day, night-time revellers emerged from the shadows into the cool light of the dawn, drunkenly staggering home or collapsed inside a sedan chair. Covent Garden led a double life. By day, the market thrived. Stallholders cried out, advertising their wares: 'Eightpence a pound, fair cherries,' 'Green hastens, fresh gathered peas,' 'Sweet lavender, six bunches a penny.' Wives, housekeepers, and busy maidservants with their baskets on their arms jostled as they haggled for a good price. Grubby street urchins ran between people's legs, waiting for the chance to steal a morsel or scoop up stray treats that had dropped, carelessly, to the ground. Set underneath the arches of the piazza which ran around the perimeter of the market were small shops, drinking dens, and kiosks. Men absent-mindedly glanced at the scene from the windows of coffee houses like the Bedford, where actors and artists gathered.

By the late afternoon, the market stalls had packed up for the day and the atmosphere darkened in anticipation of the coming night. Carriages arrived, setting down gentlemen and ladies in confections of lace, satin, and embroidery. Jewels twinkled momentarily, caught in the blaze of a torch carried by one of the linkboys who ran ahead of the sedan chairs that shuttled back and forth. The area's evening trade was entertainment, the theatre, drinking, gambling, and sex. Covent

Garden was notorious for prostitution, with two-thirds of London's brothels and bawdy houses situated in its precincts. Over the years, both the original open-air market and the surrounding streets had fallen into disrepute. Rakes, wits, and playwrights moved into the area.

This, then, was Kitty's world, neither one thing nor another but with many paths opening up before the young girl. A steadying parental influence might have directed her towards a route leading to stolid and secure – if dull – respectability. Mr Fischer had aspirations of grandeur, however, at least on Kitty's behalf. Of all his children, she was the apple of her father's eye. John Henry Fischer spared no expense in his ambitions. Kitty, as a child, was dressed up like a lady of fashion, in miniature. She looked like an aristocrat's daughter, rather than a tradesman's. Whatever objections Kitty's mother might have had to this were overruled.

Anne Fischer could, perhaps, foresee the pitfalls more clearly than her husband. It may have been Anne's influence that led to Kitty being placed, for a time, beyond the sole control of her father. If Kitty was going to climb the social ladder, then her education could not be neglected, and on this point both her parents agreed. With a little scrimping and saving, they managed to pay for a place at a small boarding school in Hammersmith. Kitty was probably around six years old when she was enrolled there. As well as the basics of education, Kitty was taught etiquette and good manners. She was given lessons in speaking French and received tuition in dancing and music. Her besotted father was intent on Kitty marrying upwards, even if he missed her being at home. He knew that a good school would add the necessary polish to his favourite daughter. It would lift Kitty above her peers. At the very least, John Henry and Anne Fischer hoped that education and the acquisition of pretty manners would help Kitty find a genteel occupation. A governess, perhaps, or a lady's companion? Without a doubt, Kitty received a good education. She was witty, always known as a good conversationalist. Moreover, she was elegant, both in appearance and in her manners. There were no rough edges to Kitty. She was polished to perfection. Other women who shared Kitty's later profession were described as coming from London's slums. They were flower girls or streetwalkers before becoming courtesans. In contrast, Kitty's childhood was respectable and she had been brought up to be ladylike. She was no common tradesman's daughter.

It was concern for Kitty's health that put an end to her schooldays. When she returned to Soho after being at her boarding school for seven years, Kitty was thin and pale. She was suffering from an illness known as 'the green sickness', or chlorosis, and the Fischers were alarmed. Death came all too easily and often with scary suddenness. London's smoggy, smoky air was unhealthy. Kitty's parents knew that her best chance of recovery would be for their daughter to live away from her home once again. She had to be sent back into the country and her recovery entrusted to strangers. An establishment was found which catered for invalids. It was located in Paddington, then a rural village on the outskirts of London.

The green sickness was also called the virgin's disease and was particularly problematic in girls who had just reached puberty. Historically, doctors had been unsure of the cause. The name was given because the skin paled to such a degree that it took on a green hue and lethargy and weakness were common symptoms. The salacious writer who recorded Kitty's girlish illness blamed female masturbation and sexual frustration for causing the disease. He was not alone in his thinking. The libertine Giacomo Casanova believed so too. He said: 'I do not know, but we have some physicians who say that chlorosis in girls is the result of that pleasure indulged in to excess.' Some people – predominantly male – went further and believed that sexual activity would cure the illness.

Thankfully, there were others with more common sense. Hannah Woolley, who had written on household management and medical matters in the seventeenth century, had a simpler, more practical remedy. She recommended young girls were kept busy and prescribed currants steeped in claret with rosemary and mace. It is now believed that girls suffering from the ailment were anaemic. Some doctors of the period had begun to suspect this was the cause and prescribed an iron-rich diet. Possibly Kitty was treated by one of these enlightened doctors who sent his patient into the countryside to recover. The house in Paddington was far enough distant from the capital that the air was fresh and clean, and that would have benefited Kitty. The actor John Henderson later recalled Kitty's kindness to his elder brother while she was at Paddington. Henderson's brother had been a copperplate engraver's apprentice in London. He was taken ill (probably with tuberculosis, known in the eighteenth century as consumption) and sent from the city to the same house where Kitty lodged. When she heard the boy's hacking coughs, she went into his room to see if she could help. John Henderson said that Kitty cradled his brother, and the lad died in her arms.[3]

Kitty was fortunate. She recovered and returned to Soho full of health and with her schooldays at an end. Kitty was around 14 or 15 and, in the mid-eighteenth century, this was old enough for her to be viewed as a young woman. On her arrival back in Soho, she piqued the curiosity of men about town. Still naïve in the ways of the world, Kitty was considered by London's rakes as easy prey. A contemporary writer imagined a predatory conversation between two men who had noticed Kitty:

'Who is that girl?'
'She is a new face.'
'Is she upon the town?'
'No.'
'What, a girl of fortune?'
'No.'
'Where does she live?'
'With her father.'
'Oh, then we shall soon have her.'[4]

The same writer who recorded that conversation said that one roguish man determined to do just that, to 'have' Kitty, whether she liked it or not. He was wealthy, with the means, so he thought, to procure a young girl for an evening as if she, and her virginity, were a commodity to be bought and sold. It was a business transaction, but Kitty would have no say in the bargain to be struck. This man sought out someone even more depraved than himself. Jack Harris was London's self-proclaimed Pimp Master General and head waiter at the Shakespeare's Head Tavern in the north-eastern corner of Covent Garden's Piazza. Next door to this tavern stood a brothel run by Mother Jane Douglas. Harris (whose real name was John Harrison) existed in the shadows of London's seedy underbelly. He was a rogue and supplemented his income by acting as a go-between for the brothels, the prostitutes, and their would-be customers. Kitty's admirer offered Harris £100 to procure the young girl and deliver her to him. It would not be the first nor the last time Harris had brokered such a deal.

John Henry Fischer fell an unsuspecting dupe to the silver-tongued Harris. To gain access to Kitty, Harris contrived to bump into her father at a tavern and got him drunk. He turned Mr Fischer's head with stories of the great match he could make for his pretty, well-mannered daughter. Harris confided that Kitty had a rich admirer who was a 'man of strict honour'. Of course, it was all lies, but Kitty's gullible father fell for them. Harris's words were music to his ears; to have Kitty married to a wealthy gentleman would achieve everything he wanted for his daughter. With more mercurial self-interest, it would also be of benefit to John Henry Fischer himself. His income was nowhere near what it once had been, and he had squandered a small fortune on Kitty. Might a son-in-law with plenty of cash be induced to spread his wealth around Kitty's wider family, wondered Mr Fischer? After all, he reasoned, if the man who desired his daughter was honourable as well as rich, then what could go wrong?

A plan was hatched. Jack Harris would invite the man who wanted Kitty to his house, to spend the evening there. Meanwhile, John would suggest to Kitty that she dropped in to call on Harris's wife, on the night in question. If we are to believe the account in a pseudo-biography of Kitty's life, written about four years later, Kitty did just that. After knocking on the door, she was invited into the house by a woman she thought was Mrs Harris. In reality, Harris was not married and the woman was a 'common strumpet' who had been hired for the night's deception. The trusting and innocent Kitty was asked to sit on a sofa while 'Mrs Harris' fussed about, lighting candles and straightening cushions before excusing herself to go and fetch a pot of tea. Kitty sat waiting for her new friend to return but, when the door opened, a strange man stood there. He entered, and the door banged shut behind him.

Kitty was alone with the man who had paid Jack Harris to bring her there. He rushed at her and pushed a purse heavy with coins into Kitty's pocket, despite her protestations. Kitty was now bought and paid for, or so the man thought. Kitty had other ideas. She refused to let herself be taken by force. Screaming, she struggled out of the man's hold and off the sofa. Kitty ran to the sash window. Throwing it up, she took a lungful of air and bellowed 'murder' as loud as she could. A crowd gathered outside and Jack Harris decided enough was enough. Before the mob could storm his house to rescue Kitty, he burst into the room. Pretending to be shocked, Harris attempted to calm Kitty while berating her would-be rapist. He called for the pot of tea, which still hadn't arrived, but Kitty refused to stay a second longer and ran home to tell her father what had happened. John Henry Fischer was furious and on the point of storming round to Harris's house when Kitty discovered the purse in her pocket. His eyes narrowed as he saw the flash of gold inside, and he paused before counting out the coins. They amounted to over £50, the equivalent of a year and a half's wages. Rather than have to return this windfall, Kitty's father decided the matter was closed. However, Mr Fischer kept a closer eye on his daughter, making her a prisoner in her own home for a while.

The whole episode is reminiscent of Charlotte Spencer's misfortunes. Charlotte was the daughter of a Newcastle coal merchant. Beautiful and well-educated, she was noticed by a peer's son, who paid Harris to go north and bring her back. Jack Harris managed to get introduced to Charlotte. He pretended to be a gentleman, and in love with her himself. Charlotte soon fell under his spell. She eloped with Harris and, once in London, married him in a private ceremony that – she later realised – had no legal basis. On the wedding night, however, Charlotte did not yet suspect that anything was wrong. She was grateful to her new husband when he let her get ready for bed in private. Once the candles had been snuffed and the room was in darkness, he entered, lifted the covers, and slid into the bed beside her. It wasn't until dawn that Charlotte saw the man she had spent the night with was not the man she had married. The man who had spent the night enjoying her body was a stranger and, she discovered, the rogue who had paid Harris to procure her. It was said that 'out of bed [Charlotte] flew, and with the utmost rage called murder! villains! but there were no servants, no persons to answer [her] call.'

Alone in London, and ruined, Charlotte had no choice but to become the man's mistress. After a while, he tired of her. Never one to waste an opportunity, Harris came to Charlotte's dubious rescue and put her onto his list of prostitutes, whom he pimped out. This list formed the basis for a notorious directory of London's sex workers, *Harris's List of Covent-Garden Ladies* (or *A Man of Pleasure's Kalendar*). It was first published in 1757, and annually thereafter to 1795. This scurrilous and sordid pocketbook was a kind of trade directory for the city's whores and courtesans. It gave 'an exact Description of the most celebrated Ladies of Pleasure who frequent Covent-garden and other Parts of this Metropolis'. Although *Harris's List* bore his name, and the earlier ones certainly made use of his list of prostitutes, Jack Harris was not the author. That was a man named Samuel Derrick, a newspaper hack and would-be playwright who was a good friend to many ladies of ill-repute. Kitty would later get to know Derrick and merit inclusion in at least one edition of the list but at least, for now, she had escaped the same fate as poor Charlotte Spencer.[5]

Around this time, Kitty received a marriage proposal. It offered her the prospect of a lifetime of security. Little did Kitty know that this proposal represented a crossroads in her life, for two paths now lay before her. The offer of marriage came from one of Kitty's neighbours, a lad around her age. He was not the type of man Kitty wanted, though. Kitty's suitor was no gentleman, he was just a tradesman's son, honest and sincere but a little dull. His father was a pewterer, albeit a wealthy one. The lad wrote to Kitty, asking for her hand. It was a sensible letter that set out what he could offer but lacked any great passion. Kitty showed the letter to her father and they thought the same thing: Kitty was worth more. She wrote back, using her father as an excuse and telling her suitor that he had forbidden the match. In doing so, Kitty took the first steps on the road that led to a different life altogether.

By the age of 15, Kitty was working. She was either a milliner, working from her home, or employed as a milliner's apprentice. In the 1750s, milliners were concerned with more than making hats, caps, and bonnets. Their shops provided needlework, quilted petticoats (together with the requisite hoops), and also lace, ribbons, gloves, and, as one commentator put it, 'as many etceteras as would reach from Charing Cross to the Royal Exchange'. John Henry Fischer, an artisan craftsman, thought millinery a good profession for his daughter. It was an occupation that personified glamour and so Kitty's pretty face and dainty airs and graces made her well suited. A milliner needed to be well-dressed, well-mannered, and – above all – attractive. Milliners' apprentices were walking adverts for their employer; they dressed to turn heads every day.

In the course of her work, a milliner gained an intimate acquaintance with her social superiors and this was not without its dangers, or advantages, depending on how you viewed the matter. Although most customers were women, men also frequented millinery shops to buy lace and decoration for their outfits, and gifts for the women in their lives. Sometimes, they came into the shop with the sole intention of flirting with the staff. A pretty milliner was as much a draw for her male clientele as the goods she sold, perhaps even more so. Thus, the profession of milliner, like that of a dressmaker, had both respectable and disreputable connotations. The two occupations were often used as a 'polite' byword for prostitution. In 1747, the author of the *London Tradesman* warned parents about the dangers of millinery:

> Out of Regard to the Fair Sex, I must caution parents, not to bind their Daughters to this Business: The vast Resort of young Beaus and Rakes to Milliner's Shops, exposes young Creatures to many Temptations, and insensibly debauches their Morals before they are capable of Vice. A young Coxcomb no sooner is Master of an Estate, and a small Share of Brains, but he affects to deal with the most noted Milliner… Thus the young Creature is obliged every Day to hear a Language, that by degrees undermines her Virtue, deprives her of that modest Delicacy of Thought, which is the constant Companion of uncorrupted Innocence, and makes Vice become familiar to the Ear, from whence there is but a small Transition to the grosser Gratification of the Appetite… Nine out of ten of the young Creatures that are obliged to serve in these Shops are ruined and undone: Take a Survey of all common Women of the Town, who take their Walks between *Charing-Cross* and *Fleet-Ditch*, and, I am persuaded, more than one Half of them have been bred Milliners, have been debauched in their Houses, and are obliged to throw themselves upon the Town for want of Bread, after they have left them. Whether then it is owing to the Milliners, or to the Nature of the Business, or to whatever

Cause is owing, the Facts are so clear, and the Misfortunes attending their Apprentices so manifest, that it ought to be the last Shift a young Creature is driven to.[6]

The eighteenth-century artist William Hogarth depicted an opposite view of the profession in his series of genre paintings, *A Rake's Progress*. Hogarth's two sisters were milliners, so he had a vested interest in promoting the trade as a respectable one. In the journey through the eight paintings, the fictional Sarah Young is abandoned by the eponymous 'rake', her lover Tom Rakewell, when he comes into a fortune. Pregnant and with no other means of support, Sarah turns to the millinery business. By dint of hard work, she turns her life around and attempts to save Tom as he plunges headfirst towards his ruin. However, others in the public eye perpetuated the idea that milliners were synonymous with the sex industry, agreeing with the author of the *London Tradesman*. A few years earlier, John Cleland had published his novel, *Memoirs of a Woman of Pleasure*, now better known as *Fanny Hill*. Fanny, an orphan who was the same age as Kitty, arrived in London seeking work. She fell into the clutches of Mrs Cole, a bawd who operated a brothel fronted by a millinery business. The novel describes how:

In the outer parlour, or rather shop, sat three young women, very demurely employ'd on millinery work, which was the cover of a traffic in more precious commodities; but three beautifuller creatures could hardly be seen. Two of them were extremely fair, the eldest not above nineteen; and the third, much about that age, was a piquant brunette, whose black sparkling eyes, and perfect harmony of features and shape, left her nothing to envy in her fairer companions. Their dress too had the more design in it, the less it appeared to have, being in a taste of uniform correct neatness, and elegant simplicity. These were the girls that compos'd the small domestick flock, which my governess train'd up with surprising order and management, considering the giddy wildness of young girls once got upon the loose.[7]

The innocent Fanny Hill's virginity was a coveted prize for Mrs Cole, who sold it to the highest bidder and, in the process, immured Fanny into the world of prostitution. Fanny was later rescued from Mrs Cole's 'millinery' by her lover, Charles, a customer at the house. However, she was then left to fend for herself when his family – horrified by Charles's liaison with a woman they viewed as a common whore – mounted a deception and sent him overseas. While Fanny Hill might have been fiction, it had parallels in the real world. Dorothy Clement was the daughter of a County Durham postmaster who was discovered sitting in a dustcart outside the Bishop of Durham's door by a clergyman's wife. This woman later said of Dorothy that even 'in all her rags and dirt, she never saw a more lovely creature'. Dorothy was apprenticed to a Covent Garden milliner-cum-bawd who 'transferred her to Neddy W, who doated on her till the day of her death'. Neddy W. was Edward Walpole, one of the younger sons of the First Lord of the Treasury (the position we know today as prime minister), Sir Robert Walpole of Houghton Hall in Norfolk. Although Edward and Dorothy never married, they lived as man and wife at Windsor's Frogmore House and had four children together.[8]

At this distance in time, it is impossible to know if Kitty's place of employment was similar to the fictitious Mrs Cole's shop. Was it a front for a bawdy house, or a genuine business making hats for the capital's fashionable and wealthy clientele? A near-contemporary writer said that Kitty operated on her account, from her father's Soho house. If that is true, then Kitty's business was more than likely an honest one. Even so, her father must have known about the risks associated with the millinery business for a naïve young girl. He gambled that one of the gentlemen who visited might fall in love with Kitty and hoped that the benefits would outweigh any risks. John Henry Fischer set up his daughter in the room which had once been his workshop, where he had engraved designs onto silverware. Keeping Kitty in the style to which she had fast become accustomed had near enough bankrupted her father. His trade had declined (due in part to a tax on the possession of silver plate) but his expenses, as they concerned Kitty, remained high.

Without enough work to carry on his own business, Mr Fischer became a jobbing tradesman, accepting work from other employers as and when he could. As a result, his workshop in the family home lay empty. Kitty's father acted in what he considered was the best way to secure his daughter's future. He turned that space into Kitty's millinery shop. Regardless of any other factors, the Fischer family now needed Kitty to bring some much-needed income into the house. From that time forward, except for a year or two, Kitty would be her family's main breadwinner. She had to be resourceful. With employment opportunities for women limited, John Henry Fischer baulked at the idea of seeing Kitty reduced to working as a servant. Millinery provided an opportunity for his smart daughter to keep in touch with the fashionable world around her, to see and be seen. At the same time, Mr Fischer had not forgotten Jack Harris's attempt to ensnare Kitty in a mire of sin. If she was under the same roof as her father, then he could keep an eye on her, or so he thought. Despite that, did John still hope that a wealthy gentleman would visit the shop, spy Kitty, fall in love with her, and whisk her away, into matrimony? Undoubtedly he did. Mr Fischer – and probably Kitty herself – viewed the milliner's shop as a temporary stepping-stone. Kitty dreamed about a life of luxury and a place in London's high society. She wanted to be the other side of the counter, trying on and buying hats, not making and selling them.

For a time, it must have seemed that a future as a lady of fashion was within her grasp. Word spread about the pretty new milliner and Kitty's shop was visited by an increasing number of men about town. They played the role of lovestruck admirers, dripping honeyed compliments into the ears of the naïve girl who stood behind the counter. Would

Kitty have realised that, far from thinking about marriage, these men were vying with one another to claim her virginity? She was young and impressionable but, whatever her father's care of her and his once strict Lutheran faith, Kitty had grown up alongside London's Covent Garden. Vice had always been just a hop, skip, and a jump away from her Soho home. However much her parents tried to shelter her from the real world, Kitty was not innocent of the ways of men. However, for a while, nothing went beyond coquettishness and harmless flirting. Then, one day, a dark-haired, handsome army officer made Kitty's acquaintance and everything changed in an instant. She fell head over heels in love with him, with all the impetuosity of her youth.

Anthony George Martin was eleven years older than Kitty and an officer in the Coldstream Guards. When he captured Kitty's heart, Martin was a newly commissioned lieutenant in the regiment. The natural-born son of an English merchant who traded in Portugal, Martin had been born in Lisbon. His mother was a Portuguese woman, known only as Martha. As he strutted the London streets in his military uniform (a red coat with blue and white facings and tight blue breeches), Martin lapped up the attention. His olive complexion contrasted deliciously with his powdered wig, worn under a black tricorn hat, and he was known by one and all as a ladies' man. Anthony George Martin's contemporaries nicknamed him 'the Military Cupid', and Kitty was far from being his first conquest. When he set eyes on her, Martin was in a relationship with an auburn-haired Irish beauty named Mrs White. This lady had a chequered past and was soon abandoned when Martin set his sights on Kitty.

Their first tryst came about when Kitty visited the theatre and found herself seated next to him. Martin's Mediterranean good looks turned Kitty's head. Possibly, the two had seen each other before. Perhaps, even, Martin had called into the millinery shop where Kitty worked? It's not much of a stretch of the imagination to suppose that Martin had lolled on the counter in Kitty's millinery and, with a twinkle in his eye, mentioned he was going to see the play. Nor that Kitty registered the information and determined to be there too, all tricked out in her best dress. Martin lived in Soho, in a courtyard known as Panton's Square, which was tucked away along a narrow thoroughfare leading to Coventry Street. The back of Panton Square opened onto a yard containing stabling and coach houses (Panton Stables) and then onto Windmill Street. Anthony Martin's home was not far from Kitty's on Moor Street. All that separated them was a small conundrum of streets and the enclosed tree-lined garden of Leicester Fields (now Leicester Square). There was ample opportunity for the two to bump into one another with increasing regularity if there was a glimmer of attraction between them.

Events moved with haste after that night at the theatre. Mrs White was given her marching orders and left to bewail her bad fortune, while Martin invited Kitty to come and live with him. She didn't need to be asked twice. Kitty packed her belongings in secret and waited for a chance to creep out, unobserved. Perhaps she feigned illness one Sunday morning and cried off going to church with the rest of her family, only for them to find her missing when they returned? Kitty was a milliner no more. Her parents were horrified at the turn of events. It was said that:

> [Martin] praised her beauty and commended her wit; she approved his person, and was not displeased with his compliments … He was charmed with the beautiful innocence of her person, and she was pleased with finding a lover in an officer, and a man of his appearance and fortune.[9]

Kitty's parents might have disapproved, but there was little they could do short of mounting a kidnap operation. If she had been spirited away by an earl, or a duke, then things might have been different. Although reasonably wealthy, Martin was just a lowly Guards officer, and he was reluctant to make Kitty his wife. In an attempt to disguise their daughter's transgression as much as possible, the Fischers told friends and neighbours that Kitty and Martin were married anyway. Perhaps they impressed on Kitty the need to keep up the pretence, for the sake of respectability? Kitty took heed of the advice, in this at least. She began to refer to herself as Mrs Catherine Martin, but there was no wedding, no matter how much Kitty and her parents wished for it. Although he may have hinted that he would, in time, make Kitty his wife, Martin had no intention of doing any such thing.

Anthony Martin's father had died a few years earlier, leaving his only child a sizeable inheritance that Martin was keen to preserve. He was no wild spendthrift. However, as far as his means allowed, Martin was living life to the full in London and enjoying having a pretty girl on his arm, to the envy of his friends. Kitty's life became a whirl of excitement. Her companions were Martin's fellow officers, and the women they consorted with. The wife of an ordinary soldier might have been happy to associate with Kitty. These women, in general, came from the middle to lower ranks of society. But Anthony George Martin was an officer, and his fellow officers' wives would be more discerning. The mistresses of those officers, though, that was another matter altogether. Alongside these 'fallen women', all escorted by their gallant men in uniform, Kitty began to be noticed at London's fashionable resorts. She visited London's pleasure gardens, the theatre, and the opera.

Kitty and her female companions were following in the footsteps of women like the once-notorious Polly Armstrong. Polly's fate should have provided a warning to Kitty. She had also been a milliner, 'in which capacity she was debauched by a young officer of the guards'. Polly's lieutenant only had his army pay to support himself, though, whereas Anthony Martin had his inheritance, thanks to his mercantile father. When Polly's lover realised that his lieutenant's wages were too meagre, he decided she needed to earn her keep. He encouraged Polly to sell herself to his brothers-in-arms. In essence, he acted as her pimp and Polly spread her favours around the regiment. Two years later, she fell ill with smallpox and although she recovered, Polly's lovely face was scarred and pock-marked and the soldiers didn't want her anymore. She appeared in at least one edition of *Harris's List* because, once abandoned by her lieutenant, Polly had no choice but to become a prostitute.

Kitty, naïvely sure of her own lover's constancy, closed her eyes and ears to any concerns. She had been given an intoxicating glimpse of a glamorous life, one which lay so close that she could almost take hold of it. Almost, but not quite. Despite Kitty's love for him and her desire to be a perfect wife (even if there had been no ceremony), the good life at Anthony Martin's side didn't last. He was promoted to a captaincy in his regiment, was posted overseas, and Kitty was left alone. Popular legend recalls that Martin had left her money to live on, but he remained away for longer than expected, and soon Kitty had spent it all. However, perhaps the truth was a little more prosaic? Martin was noted as being a bit of a skinflint and Kitty had expensive tastes. Keeping her did not come cheap, and Martin was alarmed to see his fortune vanishing. Perhaps he considered his recall to action something of a blessing, and took the opportunity it offered to distance himself from Kitty? If so, he abandoned her, even if Kitty did not realise it at first.[10]

In the mid-1750s, England and France battled each other over disputed territory in North America. Closer to home, Prussia had been scrapping with Austria and the powerful Holy Roman Empire. Tensions soon bubbled over and spread across the globe. Prussia and some of the small German states allied with England while Austria, France and Spain opposed them. The ensuing conflict became known as the Seven Years' War. In May 1758, two years into hostilities, the Coldstream Guards sailed for the Isle of Wight. From there, they raided the French coastline and suffered casualties during the disastrous Battle of Saint-Cast in Brittany.

Anthony George Martin emerged from the action unscathed. Afterwards, the regiment returned to England, but Martin stayed away from Kitty. Instead, his roving eye latched on to a fresh target.

On 23 September 1759, at St Anne's church in Soho, Anthony George Martin brought his namesake one-day-old son to be christened. The young mother was recorded in the church's baptism register as Anne Martin but she, like Kitty before her, was pretending to be his wife. Kitty's parents still lived in Soho and the local gossips must have made sure that Kitty knew Martin now had a son. The ceremony took place in the same church in which she had been christened and where she still had friends. Even if that was Martin's parish church, to have the christening performed there seems cruel. Maybe, though, it was tit-for-tat revenge between the two ex-lovers? In the year or so since they had parted, Kitty – still no older than 18 – had become infamous as a 'celebrated' courtesan. Rather than pining for Martin, she had been catapulted into the spotlight. Was Kitty's initial foray into the life of a high-class prostitute an attempt to make Anthony George Martin jealous, or was it simply a means of survival? If there was a lack of opportunities for women in Kitty's day, then a discarded mistress had fewer options than most.

When Captain Martin returned to the capital, he discovered that Catherine Maria Fischer had become known across London as Kitty Fisher, her name a byword for immorality. Despite this, for many years, Kitty still referred to herself as Catherine Martin, keeping hold of the surname belonging to the man she had loved and lost. While she had been with Martin, Kitty had lived as a wife, even if it was in name only. She spent the rest of her life seeking to replicate that happiness. Meanwhile, Martin rose to great heights within his regiment, becoming a lieutenant-general. It seems that no other woman ever came close to replacing Kitty, for Martin never married. Perhaps Kitty was the one great love of his life, and he regretted losing her? The writer of Anthony George Martin's obituary recalled that Kitty 'retained her partiality for him during life, and was always ready to quit the most wealthy and elevated admirer for his sake'. A later chance meeting suggests that Lieutenant-General Martin never quite forgot Kitty, either.[11]

Chapter Two

The Celebrated Miss Kitty Fisher

'A hundred buys her for a night,
And who shall say she is not right?'
(*Kitty's Stream*, 1759)

For a woman who is remembered as one of history's most infamous courtesans, Kitty's career at the top of London's sex trade was surprisingly short. By the time Anthony George Martin had become a father, she had become London's first and foremost celebrity and was about to voluntarily step away into private life. It all happened with dizzying speed.

A few months earlier, Kitty had moved to the upmarket West End of London, to a house on Norfolk Street in Mayfair. Kitty's new address lay parallel with Park Lane (or Tyburn Lane as it had been known); the Tyburn gallows still stood at the northern end of Park Lane, where it met Oxford Street. Crowds would gather at the crossroads whenever an execution took place, amid almost a festival atmosphere. More pleasant diversions could be found in the parkland surrounding Kitty's new home. There one could enjoy the fresh air and stroll, ride, or be driven in a fine carriage. Hyde Park was just behind her house and Green Park and St James's Park were both close by. Beyond the parks were fields and common land. Kitty's home was in the fashionable, up-and-coming area where London's urban sprawl began to encroach into the surrounding countryside.

When Kitty moved in, building work was still underway on the neighbouring properties. It was busy, dusty, and noisy but with the promise of a smart and elegant house once the builders had moved away. At the end of the street, there was a public house, the Coach and Horses. On the eastern side, the houses were narrower, but they had larger gardens to compensate for a lack of space inside. The houses on the western side were better. They were larger, with an impressive amount of living space and they looked out from the back onto Park Lane and Hyde Park. The houses here had more compact gardens, but the view of the park made up for that; they were more expensive and, therefore, more desirable. Kitty lived in one of these, with a view of Hyde Park. Nothing, it seemed, was too good for London's newest sensation. The gentlemen who lined up to pay court to Kitty had deep enough pockets to allow her to live in a grand style to which, she was determined, she would become accustomed. Already notorious among the men who visited the capital's gentlemen's clubs and coffee shops, now the world at large was about to be introduced to Kitty Fisher.[1]

It was, however, a big leap to go from the discarded mistress of a junior officer in the Guards to a high-class courtesan. What had happened to propel Kitty from obscurity to the threshold of a new existence? The answer – although it seems bizarre – lies within the pages of the diarist Fanny Burney's *Memoirs* and a late eighteenth-century biography of Dr Samuel Johnson written by his friend, William Boswell. Both Dr Johnson and Fanny Burney tell a tale about Bet Flint, a woman who became Kitty's friend.

Elizabeth 'Bet' Flint was a 'woman of the town' and, according to Dr Johnson, a slut, drunkard, whore, and thief. She was also beautiful and possessed of intellect and education. Fanny Burney recalled how Dr Johnson had told her, 'Oh, I loved Bet Flint!' Bet had managed to secure well-furnished 'genteel lodgings, a spinet [harpsichord] on which she played, and a boy that walked before her [sedan] chair.' Having a personal link boy, who would light the way home by walking in front holding a lighted torch, was a measure of personal safety if you could afford the expense. Hired link boys all too often had connections with London's criminal gangs and would lead the sedan chairmen into an ambush by thieves. In Bet's case, however, Dr

Johnson was probably giving a nod to a famous actress and courtesan-turned-bawd of twenty years earlier.

Betty Careless had owned a brothel in Covent Garden's Little Piazza and employed a small cross-eyed boy known as Little Cazey to light her way. Both Betty Careless and Little Cazey (really Laurence Casey) were immortalised by the French engraver Louis Peter Boitard when he worked in London. His print, 'The Covent Garden Morning Frolic', sees the pair, worse for wear, returning home after a night of revelry. Given Dr Johnson's opinion of Bet's character, it's hard to imagine that she acquired her semi-affluent lifestyle without some immoral chicanery. Samuel Johnson was around 50 at this point, a prolific writer, poet, critic, playwright, and biographer, and the creator of the first ever British dictionary. He was a convivial man with many friends, both male and female. This still doesn't explain how he had got to know Bet Flint, but he referred to Bet and her comrades as his 'dear acquaintances' and said that he 'couldn't help but be glad to see them'. He and Bet knew each other well enough that she brought a literary work of her own to Johnson's house, an entertaining account of her life written in verse. She wanted Johnson to write a preface to it. The opening lines were:

> When nature first ordained my birth,
> A diminutive I was born on earth:
> And then I came from a dark abode,
> Into a gay and gaudy world.[2]

In September 1758, Bet found herself in the dock of the Old Bailey. She was charged with stealing a counterpane (quilt) and sundry other items. These were taken, it was alleged, from her lodging, a room in a house on Meard Street. (In the court transcript, Bet's address was given as Meard's Court, its earlier name.) The house in which she lodged was located in a narrow street that had formerly been a courtyard, but which had been redeveloped into a thoroughfare.

It linked Dean Street and Wardour Street in Soho. Bet's home was no distance at all from Panton's Square where Anthony Martin and Kitty had lived.

There was also a military link to Kitty's former lover. The house in Meard Street was owned by Captain John Baldwin. At the time of Bet Flint's trial, he was in Germany. Just like Anthony George Martin, Captain Baldwin saw action during the Seven Years' War. He served in the newly numbered 67th Regiment of Foot and, that summer, his regiment had left their base on the Isle of Wight, from where they had been skirmishing along the French coastline, to travel to Germany. Captain Baldwin did not know when, or even if, he would return to London and so he had left his home in the care of his trusty servant, Mary Walthow. Captain Baldwin had told Mary that, if she needed money, she was to either sell the household items or use them in furnishing rooms to rent out, as she saw fit. She had done the latter and at the beginning of August, Bet Flint had taken one of these rooms at five shillings a week. Ten days or so later, Bet ran into trouble. Mary accused her of theft and Bet was arrested and thrown into jail until her trial. The arrangement between Captain Baldwin and his servant must have been a verbal one because Mary Walthow couldn't prove ownership of the disputed goods. Unable to establish the facts, the Chief Justice (who 'liked a wench', according to Dr Johnson) threw the case out of court and acquitted Bet of all charges. She was delighted, saying, 'Now that the counterpane is my own, I shall make a petticoat of it.'[3]

It is known that Anthony Martin had provided lodgings for Kitty at an address just a few streets away from her father's home in Soho. Around this time, John Henry Fischer, his wife, and their younger children were still living on Moor Street. This was closer to Meard Street than to Panton Square. Could Martin have given up his old lodgings and taken a room for Kitty in the same house as Bet Flint when he was ordered abroad? Is it too far-fetched to imagine that Bet was moving in the same social sphere as Kitty? Perhaps not, for Dr Johnson had one more revelation to make, as Fanny Burney recounted. Bet Flint did indeed know Kitty and brought her to Samuel Johnson's home, planning to introduce her pretty young friend to the literary behemoth. To Dr Johnson's everlasting regret, he was out when they called and neither Bet nor Kitty ever repeated the visit. With Captain Martin absent and his return uncertain, Bet Flint might well have acted as an instructor for her young friend, who had been left high and dry. Was it Bet Flint who introduced Kitty to a career in London's sex trade?[4]

There was a hierarchy within the eighteenth-century sex industry. At the bottom were the unfortunate women who had to work on the streets, the prostitutes who conducted their business in alleyways and hidden courtyards. They were poor, often from the slums and addicted to drink. If they were lucky, these women might scrape together a few pennies with which they could rent a room and then they at least had some privacy. Pimps like Jack Harris took advantage of their situation, and also took a cut of their earnings. To work in one of the capital's many brothels, or bagnios, offered more in the way of security. However, the women who worked there were beholden to the bawd who ran the establishment. Once this madam had provided clothes, food, and lodging, she expected her girls to repay their expenses from the meagre amount allowed to them as wages. They were hard-pressed to free themselves from their servitude.

Even in the establishments visited by aristocratic gentlemen, the women employed there had little freedom. The bawd kept them under her control, never quite allowing them to pay back all they owed. Escape was all but impossible for many until age or disease caught up with them and then, no longer desirable, they were thrown onto the streets. At the top of the hierarchy were the women who allowed themselves, in eighteenth-century parlance, to be 'kept'. In contrast with the others of their profession, a woman like this, known as a courtesan, had more freedom, and – in some but not all cases – a level of independence. There was also the opportunity to make considerably more money than the women lower down on the sex scale. Kitty was never a streetwalker, nor did she work in any of London's brothels. She was from the beginning a courtesan, but to have accomplished that, Kitty would have needed to learn from women like Bet Flint. Kitty had to know not only how to please a man, but also how to play the game, increasing his desire and her desirability. She had to create an image and have a certain style.

While Kitty's abilities had been adequate thus far for her life as the pseudo-Mrs Martin, she lacked one necessary skill if she was going to pass for a lady of high fashion. Kitty could not ride a horse, and here Bet Flint was no use at all. The problem was soon solved. The affable and gregarious Richard (Dick) Berenger (a man who was the standard of true elegance, according to Dr Samuel Johnson) was employed to teach Kitty to ride. It was the first step on Kitty's reinvention of herself, and an expense that would repay her tenfold.[5]

Well connected (Dick's father was a London merchant and his mother was the daughter of a baronet and the sister of a viscount), Berenger was handsome and popular. He was everybody's favourite. Everyone except the bluestocking, Hannah More, that is. She described Dick as 'all chivalry, and blank verse, and anecdote'. Although he strove for success in a literary way, with the publication of some works of poetry, Dick Berenger is best remembered for his translation from the French of the two volumes of *A New System of Horsemanship*, by Claude Bourgelat. It was Dick's skill as a horseman that would later save him from a debtor's prison. His style of living was in direct opposition to his paltry income and his fortune soon vanished.

In 1760, a couple of years after he had taught Kitty to ride, Berenger was appointed the king's Gentleman of the Horse, a salaried position beneficial to the poverty-stricken Dick Berenger. As Gentleman of the Horse, Dick was the first and foremost of the king's equerries and subordinate in the stables only to the Master of the Horse (the 10th Earl of Huntingdon, at the time of Dick's appointment). In the absence of the latter, Dick had charge of all matters relating to the

King's Stables, or Mews. When the bailiffs came knocking on the door of his London townhouse, Berenger wasted no time in moving into his official residence in the Mews. There, he was safe from his creditors. Before his financial downfall, however, Richard Berenger was delighted to be asked to be Kitty's riding instructor. Horse-riding was an activity that suited Kitty's daredevil, fun-loving spirit. Pretty soon she was seen every day, galloping through Hyde Park, into Green Park and up and down the Mall. She was proud of her skill in the saddle, but perhaps Kitty should have remembered the adage: pride comes before a fall.[6]

After being abandoned by Captain Martin, Kitty was aware that she needed to waste no time in finding herself a new protector. She needed a 'keeper'. It would be a mistake to draw correlations between Kitty's world and our own. In the 1700s, a woman in Kitty's position, a fallen woman, had limited choices. Still young (she was 17), Kitty had enjoyed a taste of the high life. Full of the impetuosity and recklessness of youth, a return to her career as a milliner must have looked drab in the extreme. Likewise, begging her parents' forgiveness and asking if they could take care of her once more was tantamount to admitting her sins, and failure. If Kitty moved back into her family's Moor Street home, her expectations – at best – would be a marriage to a London tradesman. That opportunity had been presented a year or so earlier and had been turned down. No, Kitty was determined to make her way in the world and to do it on her terms.

However, if she was going to earn a living by selling her body, it would be for a price that she set and to a man of her choosing. Kitty determined to reinvent herself as a fashionable, desirable courtesan, and the horse-riding lessons had been just one part of that process. There were already several male admirers who had noticed the attractions of the new girl on the town, and they clamoured for Kitty's attention. She reckoned that, if she was able to pick which man would 'keep' her, then she had at least a modicum of control over her destiny. It was an arrangement that was all too common at the time. A man who kept a courtesan was expected to provide furnished lodgings, the more fashionable and expensive the better. If possible, he would also buy or hire his mistress a coach and four, and pay for clothes and jewellery, as well as provide an allowance for food and servants. The more money he lavished upon her, the greater the outward sign of his wealth. She was a status symbol. In return, the 'kept woman' would be at the man's beck and call and provide sexual favours, but any exclusivity depended on the depths of his purse and her desirability to other men of the town. The more men that chased after Kitty, the higher her price would be and the greater the opportunity to trade up her keeper. She could also be abandoned at any time and had little security. It was a situation open to abuse, but with less danger than that faced by the women who had to solicit on the streets, or in London's many brothels.

Kitty, although attractive, was not considered a conventional beauty. Her eyes, however, were captivating. The diarist, Hester Thrale thought them 'a Species quite apart ... their Colour was of a Sky Blue, like a Ribbon, I never saw so beautiful a Brilliant Blue; the Expression was less peculiar, but the Colour was truly Celestial.' It was Kitty's character that made her stand out from the other women of her day, her quick wit and charming manners. She was a chatterbox, but also intelligent enough to hold her own in any conversation. Kitty loved being outdoors, walking and riding, and had youth on her side. Exuberant and playful, she had no vulgarity about her. Only a select few gentlemen made it through Kitty Fisher's bedroom door. Most were kept at arm's length, granted the privilege of spending time in her company only in return for favours and gifts. The smoke-and-mirrors will-she-won't-she charade heightened their desire, and, as Kitty well knew, her value. She was – in the eyes of the gentlemen who aspired to her affections – an ideal companion both in and out of the bedroom.

Determined that she would not allow herself to fall in love again, Kitty assessed the men queuing up before her with a calculating eye.

Which of them would provide the best return, financially and in terms of status? Kitty understood that to play this game, she had to harden her heart and treat this as a business transaction. It was not something that came easily to her. Kitty craved romance, but now was not the time to indulge in such a luxury. Her scrutinising gaze settled first on Thomas Hutchings. Handsome and still a young man (he was in his early thirties), Hutchings was the rich and rakish heir to a Somerset landowner and well known for his weakness when it came to the fairer sex. Some years earlier, he had pursued a woman Kitty viewed as her rival: Maria, Countess of Coventry.[7]

Maria's parents were John Gunning of Castle Coote in County Roscommon, Ireland and the Honourable Bridget Bourke, daughter of the 6th Viscount Mayo. Despite their aristocratic connections, the family were so poor that it was rumoured Bridget considered putting Maria and her younger sister, Elizabeth, on the stage. Ultimately, an acting career was not to be the sisters' destiny. However, Bridget utilised her connections in the theatre when it came to dressing her two pretty daughters for a ball at Dublin Castle. Tom Sheridan, the Irish-born actor and manager of the Dublin theatre, loaned Maria (then around 15) and Elizabeth the costumes worn by the actresses who had played Juliet and Lady Macbeth in recent productions. The Gunning sisters made such an impression on William Stanhope, 1st Earl of Harrington and Lord Lieutenant of Ireland, that they gained his patronage.

With a pension granted to their mother, the trio travelled to England where the sisters found themselves in demand by London's high society. Maria was notorious for tactlessness, but her innocence led people to think it a charming trait. She was once introduced to the elderly King George II, who asked Maria what spectacle she would most like to see. He was referring to London's attractions and wasn't expecting Maria's reply. Without pausing to think, Maria said that she would love to witness a coronation, leaving the ageing king open-mouthed with surprise. Of course, the great gossip and letter-writer,

Horace Walpole had an opinion on the sisters (he had an opinion on everything and everybody). He said that 'these are two Irish girls, of no fortune, who are declared the handsomest women alive. I think their being two so handsome and both such perfect figures is their chief excellence, for singly I have seen much handsomer women than either.' The sisters' notoriety attracted attention wherever they went. Walpole continued by noting that the sisters couldn't 'walk in the Park, or go to Vauxhall, but such mobs follow them that they are generally driven away.'[8]

Maria Gunning had turned up her nose at the eager Tom Hutchings. Something of a 'catch', Tom stood to inherit Ven House in Milborne Port, Somerset, the property of his maternal uncle, Thomas Medlycott, together with his uncle's fortune. However, no title would come with the estate, and Maria had her sights set on a peerage. Here, the Gunning sisters' aristocratic connections proved invaluable, and they captured the hearts of two of the most eligible peers in the realm. In March 1752, Maria Gunning married George William Coventry, 6th Earl of Coventry. A month earlier, her sister Elizabeth had married the 6th Duke of Hamilton in a secret ceremony at the notorious Mayfair Chapel. It is said that the marriage was carried out in such haste that the duke had to slip a bedcurtain ring onto the bride's finger, in the absence of a wedding band.

Poor Kitty, without fortune or influential friends, had to make do with the Countess of Coventry's cast-off. Although that may have rankled, Kitty enjoyed her time as Tom Hutchings's mistress despite his reputation. He was described as 'the smoothest, greyest villain of his years'. Kitty didn't care one bit. She once more haunted London's pleasure gardens and theatres, this time on Hutchings's arm. Years later, the *Town and Country Magazine* ran one of their gossipy tête-à-tête articles, charting Tom Hutchings's sordid love life. By then, he was Thomas Hutchings Medlycott, having taken his uncle's surname after inheriting his estate and fortune. The magazine wrote that 'it was considered in the circle of gallantry a moot point whether

Captain M___n [Martin] or Mr Med___t [Medlycott] was the first who prevailed with Kitty Fisher, to commence an erratic Venus, and like other fallen stars move out of her regular vortex.'[9]

Other than the theatre and opera houses, the places to be seen in London were its pleasure gardens. Vauxhall lay on the south side of the Thames and the most popular way to gain entry to the gardens was by the river. On a summer's evening, that part of the Thames would be busy with small boats and barges ferrying pleasure-seekers to the water stairs from where Vauxhall Gardens could be accessed. Inside the grounds were woods, long promenading walks with sweet-scented plants, tents for shelter and a grove. In the centre of the grove was a banqueting room, with a portico on the front containing the orchestra. On three sides were a colonnade, into which were set open-fronted 'rooms' where small parties could sit to take refreshments. These were decorated with paintings, many by Hogarth. Thousands of globe lights illuminated Vauxhall at night. It was said that they could be lit simultaneously, turning the gardens into an instant magical fairyland. Except, that is, for the Lovers' Walk at the far end of the gardens. There the darkness prevailed, and many couples took advantage.

Vauxhall Garden's main rival was Ranelagh, twice as expensive to get in and so more refined. It was further down the Thames, next to the Royal Hospital at Chelsea, and boasted a magnificent – and huge – building at its centre known as the Rotunda. Dominating the gardens of Ranelagh, the Rotunda was an imitation of Rome's Pantheon. Inside was a contraption known as the 'fireplace' which provided warmth on a colder evening and with an immense chimney to keep the smoke away. Around the sides were forty-seven boxes where groups could be served tea and coffee. At the back of each box was a pair of folding doors that led out into the gardens. When these doors were opened, crowds could gather to stare at the occupants. Above these boxes was a covered gallery, around which Ranelagh's guests could stroll, and yet more seating areas, one of which was reserved for royalty. The orchestra was in the Rotunda's portico. The whole was lit with large bell lamps, reflected in strategically placed mirrors. Despite the concerts and masquerades – many accompanied by firework displays – the most popular amusement at Ranelagh was simply to stroll. The ladies would lean on a gentleman's arm, as they walked around the Rotunda. It was a picturesque place to see and be seen, promenading like a peacock.

Added to these two pleasure haunts was Marylebone Gardens, surrounded by a high wall. It was once a disreputable haunt of gamesters, fighters, and highwaymen but a couple of years before Kitty had burst onto the scene, Marylebone Gardens had undergone a rebrand. There was a ballroom, and around a circular walk (485 paces long, and six people wide) were fruit trees and lawns. In the centre was a bowling green, and an orchestra again played to the crowds. Breakfast, dinner, and suppers were served. The man who owned the gardens, John Trusler, was a cook, hence the focus on food. His daughter made 'Marylebone tarts', plum cakes and almond cheesecakes, the latter served hot from 1.00 pm until 3.00 pm each afternoon. While the gardens were pleasant, danger abounded on the roads leading to them, however. As Marylebone was a village set away from London's constant bustle, when the gentry and aristocracy travelled home in their carriages after an evening concert, a little the worse for wear, there was a risk of highway robbery.

Also to the north of the city, alongside the Fleet, was Bagnigge Wells on the new road which linked Paddington with Islington. A century earlier, it had been Nell Gwyn's summer residence. In 1760, two mineral springs were discovered, and Bagnigge Wells became popular as a spa as well as a tea garden. Islington Spa (or New Tunbridge Wells as it was also known) was another popular resort. In the centre was a raised basin containing the spa water, surrounded by stone balustrades and set into a lime arbour. Brick and timber buildings housed a dancing room, a coffee house and breakfasting area, and a gambling den.

Kitty let Tom Hutchings take her to all of these resorts. Then, out of the blue, and with abrupt coldness, he announced that he'd tired of Kitty. Perhaps he also found her too expensive? At any rate, Kitty was abandoned for a second time. Left high and dry by Hutchings, and with Anthony George Martin still nowhere to be seen, Kitty had no choice but to soldier on.

It was around this time that she was noticed by a Surrey landowner. Joseph Mawbey was one of the *nouveau riche*, with a background in trade. He had been taken in as a child by his uncle, a Vauxhall distiller. On his uncle's death around four years earlier, Joseph Mawbey inherited the distillery (which he ran with his cousin), a fine house, and a lot of money. Living and working at Vauxhall, Mawbey spent a lot of time in the gardens and had watched Tom Hutchings squire Kitty around with envy. Now she was without a keeper, and he saw his chance. One balmy evening, promenading at the pleasure grounds, Mawbey persuaded one of his friends to introduce him to Kitty and invited her to dine with him in one of the boxes. He regaled her with tales of his recent Grand Tour and described the sights of Paris and Rome. His words conjured images of Venetian masquerades, blue seas, and sun-drenched landscapes. In an attempt to prove to Kitty that he was a cultured gentleman despite the fact his money was from trade, Joseph Mawbey talked of the Old Masters he had viewed in European art galleries. He hoped this would be enough to entice Kitty into Vauxhall's Lovers' Walk.

Mawbey's fine speeches fell on deaf ears. Kitty wasn't impressed and made her escape. Although Mawbey tried to call on her several times afterwards, Kitty left word that she was not at home. He might have had the means to keep her, but he didn't have the social position Kitty wanted. By aligning herself with a man seen as a jumped-up tradesman, Kitty would fail to achieve the upmarket status she wanted. Kitty planned to aim a lot higher than Joseph Mawbey. If the Gunning sisters could bag themselves titles as well as wealth, then why couldn't she? As it was, Mawbey might not have been such a bad catch in the long run. After being spurned by Kitty, he married his cousin's daughter instead and bought a Surrey estate, Botleys in Chertsey. Five years after his marriage, Mawbey was granted the title of baronet. It was another moment in Kitty's life where she could have taken a different path. If Mawbey had been besotted enough to propose marriage, Kitty could have soon found herself Lady Catherine Mawbey of Botleys. Instead, she turned him away, believing it was the sensible thing to do. Although she had no crystal ball to scry the future, Kitty was trying to stick to her resolution. The reality was that she was listening to her heart more than her head and hoping to be swept off her feet.[10]

Life was now far removed from Kitty's modest upbringing in Soho, and her shady existence as Anthony George Martin's 'wife'. Kitty found herself thrust into the glare of public life, known as one of London's '*impures*'. She flirted with wealthy, titled gentlemen and debauched rakes alike. Her social circle was male-dominated and Kitty had little female company. Any woman who did spend time with Kitty was going to be someone who found themselves in a similar situation. There were a few women besides Bet Flint, however, who claimed Kitty as an acquaintance. One, who became her close friend, was Jane Sumner. She and Kitty used the same dressmaker, and that is where they met.

Jane was from a very respectable and religious family. One brother, Robert Carey Sumner, was the master of Harrow (he was known as 'the best schoolmaster in England'). A second brother, William Brightwell Sumner, was a wealthy Indian nabob who made his fortune out in Bengal working for the East India Company. Dr John Sumner, formerly Eton's headmaster and canon of Windsor, was Jane's uncle. Kitty and Jane were kindred spirits, both well-educated but with ruined reputations. They soon became inseparable. Where men were concerned, a contemporary writer put words into Jane's mouth. He claimed that she said: 'the first rule of action is to declare perpetual war against the whole sex; love no man, but fleece and gilt them all as much and as often as you can.' Though cruel, for a courtesan 'it was good advice.[11]

It was John Montagu, 4th Earl of Sandwich – a man who was a curious mix of culture, taste, learning, and debauchery – who had seduced Jane. She was his mistress when she met Kitty, and the earl kept Jane in a suitable style. Jane was a few years older than Kitty and more experienced in the ways of the world. Although Bet Flint was probably the person who introduced Kitty to a life of high-class prostitution, it was undoubtedly Jane who completed Kitty's education. It was Jane who taught Kitty how to be a successful courtesan and helped her to rise to the top. The pair modelled themselves on three society ladies of dubious character, all notorious at the time. Elizabeth Chudleigh, Lady Caroline Fitzroy, and Elizabeth Ashe formed a tight-knit group. They were known to live fast, and their morals were loose. Unlike Kitty and Jane, the aristocratic connections of these women elevated them – in varying degrees – above accusations of being a 'woman of the town'.[12]

Elizabeth Chudleigh was one of the maids of honour for Augusta, Dowager Princes of Wales. She shocked society when she appeared at a jubilee masquerade in a diaphanous dress that left little to the imagination. Her appearance resulted in a multitude of satirical prints which cemented her infamy. Elizabeth married Augustus Hervey (later the 3rd Earl of Bristol) in private. In time, she would split with Hervey and marry Evelyn Pierrepoint, 2nd Duke of Kingston-upon-Hull. Due to the secrecy of her former marriage, Elizabeth regarded it as null and void. Later, when she was found guilty of bigamy in one of the biggest scandals of the era, it was clear that Elizabeth's first marriage was all too valid.

Her friend, Lady Caroline Fitzroy, was one of the Duke of Grafton's daughters, who had a marriage that was no less difficult. She married William Stanhope, 2nd Earl of Harrington (a man who frequented London's brothels and was known as 'the goat of quality'). Despite them having seven children, Lady Caroline is thought to have been bisexual. She certainly enjoyed a reputation for scandal and was rumoured to have taken many lovers of both sexes.

The last of the trio, Elizabeth Ashe, was small and nicknamed 'Little Ashe' and also 'the Pollard Ashe'. She was rumoured to have been the illegitimately born granddaughter of George II via the king's daughter, Princess Amelia. Around a decade earlier, Elizabeth Ashe had married Lady Mary Wortley Montagu's son, Edward. The wedding was a clandestine one, conducted in the notorious Keith's Chapel in Mayfair. It was also bigamous, but this time it was the groom, and not the bride, who was at fault. Edward Wortley Montagu, a complete eccentric who had inherited his mother's love of travelling, later claimed that Elizabeth knew about his first wife, who was still alive. When still a teenager, he had married Sarah 'Sally' James in another secretive ceremony. Sally was a Covent Garden washerwoman, and Edward's family had quickly separated the pair but neglected to annul the marriage.

Intrigue, scandal, and gossip followed this riotous trio wherever they went. The circle in which they moved included Maria, Countess of Coventry. These women represented everything Kitty wished to be. However, Kitty's father was a tradesman and she had to take her place in the social hierarchy. Polite society looked down their noses at the likes of the Countess of Harrington and her coterie, and they, in turn, looked down theirs at Kitty and her friend Jane.[13]

Kitty was, however, becoming famous in her own right. Without a doubt, she enjoyed the attention, at least in the early days of her celebrity. Thomas Bowlby, a young well-connected man-about-town (his father-in-law was the 3rd Earl of Cardigan) wrote to his friend Philip Gell on 28 January 1759. Bowlby told Gell that he 'must come to town to see Kitty Fisher, the most pretty, extravagant, wicked little whore that ever flourished. You may have seen her but she was nothing till this winter.'[14]

Chapter Three

The Fisher of Men

'I believe, my dear sister, I can never say all I have to tell you – I have such numbers of things to say. Now, for news: Lord Poulett is to be married to the famous Kitty Fisher, who is really a most beautiful creature of her kind; and Lord Waldgrave is certainly to be married to Miss Maria Walpole.'

(Lady Louisa Conolly writing to the
Countess of Kildare, 10 April 1759)

It was a sign of Kitty's sudden notoriety that she was gossiped about in letters and over tea tables by aristocrats like Lady Louisa Conolly and Emily, Countess of Kildare. They were two of the four Irish Lennox sisters, daughters of Charles Lennox, 2nd Duke of Richmond, and had blue blood in their veins. The sisters were descended from King Charles II and his mistress, Louise de Kérouaille, Duchess of Portsmouth. At the beginning of the year, the wider world had started to take notice of Kitty. Just three months later, that attention had increased tenfold. By the time of the Easter weekend, it was Kitty's name that was on everyone's tongues. She was the latest sensation, and it was all because of an accident that had disastrous consequences, although not in the way that anyone might have expected.[1]

Maria Walpole, Lord Waldegrave's intended, was the granddaughter of the great eighteenth-century statesman, Robert Walpole, 1st Earl of Orford and the first Prime Minister of Great Britain. Her father was Walpole's younger son, Edward (Neddy), but Maria's parents had neglected to get married. Even worse, Maria's mother, Dorothy

Clement, was the postmaster's daughter who had been discovered sitting in a dustcart. Her illegitimacy and her mother's past might have hindered Maria's social standing. However, James Waldegrave, 2nd Earl Waldegrave, cared little for polite society's opinion of Maria Walpole's ancestry. Just as Lady Louisa Conolly predicted, a month later he did indeed marry Maria and the couple had three children together before Lord Waldegrave's death four years later. In her widowhood, the beautiful Maria, Lady Waldegrave, climbed to greater heights. Prince William Henry, Duke of Gloucester and Edinburgh and the king's younger brother, fell in love with Maria and – on 6 September 1766 in Maria's Pall Mall townhouse – married her. By doing so, the County Durham postmaster's granddaughter became the Duchess of Gloucester and Edinburgh, although it was a title she could not use straight away. The wedding was such a hush-hush affair that George III was oblivious to the fact that Maria was his sister-in-law until six years after the marriage had taken place.[2]

The man that Lady Louisa Conolly suggested Kitty was about to marry was a middle-aged bachelor who hadn't done much to trouble the world up to that point. John Poulett, 2nd Earl Poulett of Hinton St George in Somerset, was 50 years old. While his two younger brothers were MPs, Lord Poulett did little of note other than gamble and enjoy his good fortune. He was just one of the men who vied for Kitty's attention, however. After being rejected by Tom Hutchings, and spurning Joseph Mawbey, things had not gone quite to plan for Kitty. Far from acquiring a new long-lasting protector, she had, instead, found herself being passed around between several men who made up a gentleman's gambling circle. Gossip on the streets had already started to whisper that Kitty was kept by the entire club.

The first of these men to step forward as Kitty's keeper was an Irishman, Sir Charles Bingham, 7th Baronet (and later 1st Earl of Lucan). In his mid-twenties when he met Kitty, Bingham had inherited his title and fortune several years earlier while still at school after the early death of his elder brother. Coming into wealth and influence at such a young age catapulted him into life as a reckless spendthrift, and Kitty took full advantage. Bingham was smitten with Kitty from the first moment he set eyes on her. He followed her around, all puppy-dog eyes and begging her to pay attention to him. When it suited her, Kitty allowed herself to submit to the infatuated baronet's pleas, and let him offer tangible proofs of his passion. 'Did she hint she wanted a sum of money? It was immediately doubled and presented to her. Did she give the least token of desiring a footman? An equipage was provided her.'[3]

However, at this point, his largesse faltered and he baulked at providing horses to pull it. Denied her own stable, Kitty had to make do with horses that were hired, known as 'a waiting job'. It was an omission that annoyed her. In revenge, she painted Captain Martin's cypher on the carriage doors and continued to call herself Mrs Martin. One day, as this carriage rolled down one of the capital's streets, Kitty looked out of the window and saw a face she recognised. It was her old lover, Anthony George Martin, and his surprised expression, as he saw a carriage decorated with his cypher travel past, made Kitty laugh with delight. Martin watched with curiosity as the carriage ground to a halt a little further down the road. A footman was sent running from the vehicle towards the somewhat baffled Guards officer, crying out that 'his lady desired to speak with him'.

Martin strode up to the carriage and opened the door. He'd probably guessed who the occupant was by this time, but he was still flabbergasted to see Kitty inside, dressed in expensive silk and lace, her jewels glinting in the sudden daylight as he opened the carriage door. It is rumoured that, when Captain Martin set eyes on Kitty, he rediscovered his passion for her and fell, once more, into her arms. The carriage rolled off to Norfolk Street while its occupants took the chance to catch up. Touching as their reunion was, any resurgence of Kitty and Captain Martin's love affair was brief. History repeated itself when the Military Cupid's regiment was sent back abroad on manoeuvres. Kitty had no long-term success with Sir Charles

Bingham, either. After a run of bad luck at the gaming tables, Bingham decided that Kitty was an unaffordable luxury. He moved on, unable – or unwilling – to keep her any longer. In an attempt to boost his finances, Bingham instead began to look around for an heiress in need of a husband, and a title. A year later he'd found one, and married her.[4]

Sir Charles Bingham did not leave Kitty financially adrift, however. He introduced her to his equally disreputable friend, Thomas Bromley, 2nd Baron Montfort. Kitty passed from one man to the other as if she were a commodity which they traded between themselves. For Kitty, the bargain had both pros and cons. Lord Montfort was handsome, considered to look similar to the dramatist (and future manager of the Haymarket Theatre) George Colman. However, while Colman was tall and well built, Lord Montfort was a miniature version. Kitty's new keeper was an object of fun, mocked by his contemporaries due to his short stature. Like Bingham, he too was in his mid-twenties, and – in Kitty's eyes – his affluent lifestyle made up for his lack of height. It had to, for Kitty had nowhere else to turn that offered the same security.

Lord Montfort's lifestyle, however, was prone to ebb and flow according to his success at the gaming tables. A few years earlier, Montfort's father had committed suicide, shooting himself on New Year's Day 'in the morning, with all the premeditation and deliberation imaginable'. The Royal Chaplain, Edmund Pyle, wrote that the 1st Baron Montfort had 'intangled his circumstances very much, having an expensive and paltry fellow for his son, and some bodily complaints (that exercise would have cured).' It was a case of like father, like son. The 1st Baron Montfort, as with so many aristocratic gentlemen, had been a gamester and left behind a crippled estate and debts of £30,000. A year later, the 2nd Baron Montfort persuaded the prime minister, the Duke of Newcastle, to grant him a pension of £1,000 a year. When Kitty became his lover, Lord Montfort was following in his father's dubious footsteps and doing his best to get through that pension and his remaining fortune as fast as possible. It wasn't just cards he bet on either, but horse racing, cockfighting, and a myriad of obscure wagers made between his rakehell friends.[5]

Kitty soon discovered that her new protector was extravagant and wild, while his winnings lasted. He took on the role of her keeper with aplomb and spent lavishly, giving Kitty a generous allowance. She moved into a new home (it was probably Lord Montfort who acquired the Norfolk Street house for Kitty), and ordered furnishings, decorating it in style from top to bottom. Wallpaper in rich, bright colours was pasted onto the walls, the colours complemented in the silk damask window drapes. Perhaps Kitty persuaded Lord Montfort to take her to Thomas Chippendale's workshop on St Martin's Lane to choose bookcases, cabinets, armchairs, and tables? Silverware engraved by chasers, maybe even by Kitty's father, was purchased to stand upon these cabinets and tables. Kitty, via her lover's fortune, was now one of those fashionable ladies who patronised Soho's artisan craftsmen. Dismissing the much-hated 'waiting job' hired by Sir Charles Bingham, Montfort gave Kitty a new coach and loaned her his best coach horses. The house had a full complement of staff, and Kitty lived in luxury. She was just 18 years of age.

Kitty's first thought was to help her family. From the allowance given to her by Lord Montfort, she sent frequent parcels of food to her parents and gave them money too. She bought new clothes for her siblings and paid for their education. Her two sisters were sent to a boarding school and her brother to an academy. Kitty didn't forget her childhood playmates either. She employed one or two to work as upper servants in her townhouse and helped others marry their sweethearts by setting up their husbands-to-be in a trade. Kitty, kind-hearted but still naïve, did not think to save the money for her uncertain future. Lord Montfort had no intention of marrying Kitty. Just like Sir Charles Bingham, his spendthrift lifestyle necessitated a marriage to an heiress. His reputation preceded him, though and, despite his title, he was not viewed as a catch. This was all too clear to Kitty and she didn't count on anything long-lasting as far as Lord

Montfort was concerned. As a mark of some small independence, she continued to refer to herself, when asked to give her name, as Mrs Catherine Martin. She also held Lord Montfort at arm's length in other ways. Despite the cash that he threw around to impress her, Kitty was not averse to snubbing her diminutive baronet for men of greater rank, and stature.[6]

Lord Montfort was lampooned in the era's media due to his lack of height. A later account of his life included a tale that the author claimed Kitty herself used to enjoy regaling to her acquaintances. It concerned both Lord Montfort and another man who paid court to Kitty and who was both taller and higher up in the peerage than Kitty's keeper. This man was named simply as Lord S___. There is little doubt that he was John Montagu, 4th Earl of Sandwich, her friend Jane's protector. The earl was 40 years of age, intelligent, and athletic. Years before, he had married for love, but his wife's mental health deteriorated and his marriage had become one in name only. A man who enjoyed the company of women, Sandwich kept Jane Sumner as his mistress, but his eye was always inclined to rove further. The *Westminster Magazine* said of him that 'there are four things of which his Lordship is wicked enough to be very fond; these are, a cheerful company, a late hour, a good bottle, and a pretty woman.' It was inconceivable that his attention would not settle, for a while, on Kitty. After all, because of Jane, they were thrown into each other's company and often made a merry threesome.[7]

The tale, as it was told, related how Kitty was waiting at home for Lord Sandwich to arrive in his coach. They were going to the opera and, as Lord Sandwich's companion for the night, Kitty would be admitted to his box. She was dressed sumptuously in a gown with wide, hooped skirts. Before Sandwich turned up, she received a surprise – and inopportune – visit from Lord Montfort. He was shown into her rooms and as he entered, Kitty heard a carriage pull up on the street outside. She realised that hot on Montfort's heels was the eager earl and Kitty had to think quickly:

There was not a closet in her dining-room, and there was but one method left of concealing the pigmy-hero – this was beneath the fair one's hoop-petticoat. She received her second visitor with her usual ease and politeness, desired his lordship to be seated for a moment, till she retired into the adjacent apartment for her cloak, where she deposited in safety Lord M___.[8]

While other gentlemen might sometimes take Kitty to the opera, or London's parks and pleasure grounds, none of them offered anything better than her current position as Lord Montfort's mistress. Kitty would not have refused if the Earl of Sandwich asked her to accompany him for an evening. Nor, probably, if he had offered to replace Lord Montfort, as an earl was a better catch than a baron.

Kitty was quickly learning just what a precarious existence hers was. Even the elegant house on Norfolk Street was not truly hers. In return for providing the money to pay the rent, Lord Montfort used the house to throw lavish dinner parties for his friends. Of course, Kitty acted as the hostess, to the envy of Montfort's decadent coterie. The guests, except for Jane Sumner, were always male. Invariably, the night would end with gambling. London's gaming tables were the link between Bingham, Montfort, and Earl Poulett, the man whom, it was later rumoured, Kitty was about to marry. Lord Poulett was a frequent guest at Kitty's London home.

All three men were members of the upmarket White's Club in St James's Street, owned by James Arthur and also of an exclusive Faro Club. A card game of chance, Faro (or Pharaoh) originated in France in the late seventeenth century. An indeterminate number of people (punters) could play at the same time, plus a dealer, otherwise known as the banker. The game allowed the banker to win as well as the other players and was a favourite at the time. Fortunes were lost more frequently than they were won at the gaming tables, but this did not deter those who were reckless enough to gamble and risk ruination. Gentleman's clubs like White's were patronised by aristocrats and gentlemen. The most privileged members of these – those who were wealthiest or most highly titled – formed a private club-within-a-club but Faro Clubs were also often independently run affairs. George William Coventry, 6th Earl of Coventry (Maria Gunning's husband) ran a Faro bank from his country seat, Croome in Worcestershire. Perhaps Lord Montfort ran another from Kitty's home when the men were in London?[9]

Earl Poulett paid court to Kitty but, at first, it appeared nothing more than flirtation and flattery. He was a cautious man and, although a gambler, never risked more than he could afford to lose and was careful with his money. The intriguing Kitty Fisher had captivated him, however. He would often put down his cards with a sigh, and say how he wished he was twenty-five years younger while boasting of past conquests:

> Ay, my dear… at that age I should have been a match for you, at a more agreeable game than we are now playing. I was always famous for holding great cards, as the Dutchess of ___, Lady ___ and several women still living can testify. Nay, I don't think I've so entirely forgot the game, but what I should make a tolerable figure yet, with a good partner.[10]

The doughty old earl wanted Kitty but baulked at the idea of being her sole keeper. Kitty was too expensive for his parsimonious habits. No matter the depth of Lord Poulett's passion, it did not manage to outweigh his cold frugality. She had already managed to wheedle a pair of diamond earrings and £200 in cash from him, with little but her thanks in return. He was frustrated, worried that he was being played for a love-sick fool and loathe to spend more while there was no certainty of seeing a return on his gifts. Kitty was artful, keeping the penny-pinching old earl at arm's length and issuing vague promises and hints. She hoped that he would deposit more money into her hands and spend more on her at London's top jewellers.

Lord Poulett's calculating mind assessed the situation. Quickly, he came to a resolution, one oddly miserly but managing at the same time to be generous. He mentioned his plan to Kitty, who raised no objections in principle and so the earl gathered his gambling cohorts together. They met at a chocolate house; both it and White's Club with its private gambling den were homes-from-home for Kitty's men. Once Lord Poulett had assembled them he sat back and waited for the conversation to turn to Kitty's charms and her expensive tastes. When the time was right, the earl floated his grand scheme. Why didn't they, he suggested, agree to make Kitty a small allowance from their winnings? They couldn't lose, Poulett argued. They would only have to pay on those occasions that they won and, in return, all the men signed up to this contract would have an equal claim on Kitty.

Perhaps, when Kitty had given her approval, she had thought this a madcap idea that would be the joke of an hour and then fall by the wayside? Lord Poulett didn't care about the niceties. He was pleased with his bold stratagem which, he reckoned, would make Kitty beholden to him financially, albeit not exclusively. He would be able to have her without putting a strain on his finances, a part-owner in the same way that men might join together to buy a racehorse. Five members of the club agreed to Poulett's plan, but they didn't want to commit to giving away too high a stake. In the end, they pledged to give Kitty 5 per cent of their winnings. Besides Lord Poulett, these men were Sir Charles Bingham, Lord Montfort, the Earl of Coventry, and one other who remains anonymous.

The still-infatuated Bingham was keen to regain access to Kitty if he could do so at a more affordable price than before. Neither he nor Montfort was averse to sharing her favours with their friends if it saved them money. One or another of the five men would win at least £100 a day, on average, giving Kitty around £35 a week (equal to £3,000–4,000 in today's money). Lord Poulett's hare-brained scheme is the basis of the legend that Kitty was kept by the whole of Arthur's Club, as White's subsequently became known. It could also be the beginning of the oft-repeated legend that Kitty's 'price' was £100, or 100 guineas, a night. That was an enormous sum of money. A hundred pounds was the equivalent of just over three years' wages for a craftsman such as Kitty's father had once been. The legend has become half-remembered, mired in a murky truth. Kitty didn't command such fantastic sums of money, at least not yet, although she allowed the rumours to flourish, and it was not the whole club who kept her. Still, this small cohort of men could lay claim to Kitty's companionship and, if they had a winning night at the tables, to her body as well. While Kitty had little choice but to negotiate the strange set-up, she was clever enough to play them off against one another. She made her suitors compete for her attention. This in turn fired their jealousy, and their money flowed into Kitty's purse. It was a game which they all played to the hilt, despite its dubious rules.[11]

No doubt there was also an element of spite involved when Kitty allowed Lord Coventry into her bed in return for her percentage of his winnings. The earl had long since abandoned any notion of fidelity to his wife. He was a man who wanted to be at the forefront of fashion and have the best of everything. That went for his estate, his clothes, and his women. Nothing was too good for the earl. When the Gunning sisters had been the latest sensation, nobody but Maria would do. Now Kitty was the talk of the town, and so she was the woman he wanted. Although she might have wanted Lord Coventry to become her sole protector, for the earl, Kitty was nothing more than another trophy. Nevertheless, and despite this, Kitty spied an opportunity for revenge on the hoity-toity woman who looked down upon her.

The sharp rivalry between Kitty and Maria made it deliciously provocative. Before Kitty hit the headlines, Maria, Countess of Coventry was the woman every other one wanted to be. She was at the forefront of fashion, always one step ahead of her contemporaries. She led, others followed, and this rankled with Kitty. She wanted to outclass the countess. When Kitty found out that Maria had had a new and distinctive riding habit made, she pestered Lord Coventry. The countess's clothes were always individual and distinctive; she set the fashions rather than followed them. Other women had tried to emulate the riding habit and asked their dressmakers and habit makers to make one just like it. There were many imitations but none had got it quite right. Lady Coventry had an agreement with all her dress- and habit makers that they would not give up their secrets, nor make copies for anyone else.

Kitty begged, cajoled, and pleaded to be told which habit maker had made the outfit. When that didn't work, she tried a simpler method. The servants at Kitty's Norfolk Street house were ordered to refuse admittance to Lord Coventry. He would only be allowed through her front door, the footman told him, if he gave in and revealed the information that their mistress sought. Worn down, the earl relented. Despite knowing that it would reveal his liaison with Kitty to his wife, he arranged for her to have an exact copy of the habit made. Who knows, in a game of tit-for-tat revenge with his wife, Lord Coventry may have revelled in the thought of his wife's humiliation? The Coventrys' marriage had not been happy. Maria was rumoured to have taken the already married Augustus Fitzroy, 3rd Duke of Grafton as her lover and there had been suggestions that the earl was considering a divorce. However, a son (George William, the future 7th Earl of Coventry) had been born just a few months earlier.

Habit makers were male. They were tailors, rather than dressmakers, and the outfit was constructed in the same way that men's clothes were. Whatever the habit maker's misgivings at the thought of upsetting the countess, the earl demanded that an exact copy was made up for Kitty. Perhaps he claimed it was a surprise for his wife, a jest that would amuse her and her friends. The man had little choice but to comply. A few weeks later, Maria and Kitty rode past one another in Hyde Park. Lady Coventry was confident that she was the centre of attention and the picture of modish elegance in her new outfit. On any other day, Maria wouldn't have deigned to notice Kitty but, on this occasion, she stopped and stared. Kitty was wearing a riding habit identical to her own.

Masking her immediate and crippling humiliation with haughty disdain, Maria demanded to know which habit maker was responsible for Kitty's outfit. Laughing wickedly at her rival's discomfort, Kitty quipped that Maria had better ask Lord Coventry, as he had given her the outfit as a gift. The countess was horrified. Nobody spoke to her like that and, worse, her husband's contempt was now laid bare for all to see. She was reduced in an instant to a laughing stock, but Lady Coventry still tried to recover the situation. Her reply was scathing. She told Kitty that she thought her an impertinent woman. Kitty kept her cool, knowing she had the upper hand. With a theatrical sigh, and playing shamelessly to the interested eavesdroppers gathered nearby, Kitty answered the charge. She told Maria that she had no choice but to accept the insult as the countess was her social superior but that she too would marry a lord so that she could then answer back. With that, the public spat ended, but the gossip didn't. It was soon common knowledge around the capital. Giustiniana Wynne, an Anglo-Venetian woman of letters and one of Casanova's acquaintances, heard about it a year later. She recorded the information as a snippet of London tittle-tattle in one of her letters to her lover, back in Italy. For Kitty, it was yet one more step into wider public infamy and the first glimmers of the celebrity to come.[12]

The other men of the gambling club paid little attention to Poulett's flirtation with Kitty. Maybe they thought it an innocent game? After all, although only middle-aged, Poulett was perceived as old and gouty whereas the others had youth and good looks on their side. He was no Adonis. Lord Poulett did have one thing going for him, though. Despite being fond of the gaming tables, his fortune and his estate were secure and he intended to keep them so. This would not have escaped Kitty's mercurial notice. Even though she was in the joint keeping of those five gambling men, Kitty kept one eye open for a better deal. This was not how she had planned or expected events to turn out. Other men clamoured for her attention, although none stepped forward to replace the club which kept her.

Early in 1759, Kitty caught a cold. With her nose red and runny, she didn't want to be seen by anyone. While she was hidden away, it was reported that on one day alone, six peers of the realm and six members of parliament were turned away from her door. It must have frustrated Kitty that she couldn't find that one suitable protector. Being in the joint keeping of five men was not an ideal, nor a sustainable scheme. She was new to the scene and causing ripples of excitement, but they would soon abate. There were other women all eager to compete with her, and only a limited number of reprobate peers to go around. Kitty's public image needed just that little something extra to catapult her into the centre of the stage. Luckily, fate was on her side. What happened next was an event that fixed Kitty's fame and made her a household name. It may have been a publicity stunt, and Kitty was clever enough to have carried off such a preposterous scheme with style. Such a ruse would have required meticulous planning, though. It is more probable that Kitty's misadventure was a simple accident, albeit one that she was quick-witted enough to turn to her advantage.[13]

Chapter Four

A Fallen Woman, Falling

'Who rides fastest, Miss Kitty Fisher, or her gay gallant?'
(*The Merry Accident*, March 1759)

In the early March of 1759, on a sunny springtime morning, Kitty and her friend Jane Sumner were on horseback, cantering through Hyde Park. Dressed in a stylish black riding habit and sitting side-saddle on a nimble piebald horse, Kitty was the epitome of elegance. This fact was not lost on the two army officers – dressed in full uniform – who were riding with Kitty and Jane. Throwing back her head and laughing in delight, Kitty galloped towards Kensington Gardens before skirting left and following the perimeter of the park down to Constitution Hill. Her companions rode after her. The foursome cantered through Green Park and onto the Mall, heading towards St James's Park.

It was lunchtime and the Mall was busy, so Kitty slowed down. Behind wooden fences along the sides, trees lined the route, overhanging the path. A detachment of soldiers was marching to their post through the crowded thoroughfare, stamping up dust in their wake from the gravelled surface. These soldiers suddenly turned and, as they wheeled into position, Kitty's horse was startled. It bolted, and Kitty screamed in terror. People who had, seconds earlier, been promenading now scattered from the piebald horse's path. Their screams and shouts drowned out Kitty's terror, but she didn't notice. All Kitty's attention was focused on trying to stay in her saddle. Several bystanders were almost trampled beneath the horse's hooves. A couple of brave, if rash, gentlemen ran forward in a futile attempt to grab the reins. The panicked horse galloped headlong until it reached the Stable Yard where it came to a sudden halt and reared upwards, throwing Kitty to the ground. She landed in the dust and dirt with a sickening thud.

One of the officers from Kitty's party had been in close pursuit. Jumping down from his saddle, he ran to Kitty's side. Anxious crowds gathered, fearing the worst. As Kitty looked around at the concerned faces gazing down at her, she decided not to play the victim but the victor. With quick thinking, she was acutely aware that the scene presented a picturesque tableau. Kitty lay, dishevelled, in her officer's arms. Tears streamed down her face, smudging dirty streaks and making her look younger than her years, and the officer was full of anguished concern for his pretty companion.

Two years earlier, Kitty must have seen the newspaper reports of a similar accident in Hyde Park. Lady Coventry's horse had fallen 'with and upon her … whereby she was so bruised as to occasion the Blood to gush from her Mouth, Nose and Ears.' The drama left Maria lying dangerously ill. Kitty was lucky. Her accident could have had a much worse outcome but, although bruised and sore, nothing except her pride had been injured. There was no blood and gore to mar the scene. It was, Kitty realised, a chance for her to succeed where her rival had failed. With a 'pretty childishness', Kitty stopped crying and instead broke into peals of laughter, making light of her near-death experience. Someone looking on realised who she was and her name passed through the crowd, first in a whisper, then louder. 'It's the famous Kitty Fisher!' A sedan chair was commandeered and Kitty placed inside. As she was borne in a triumphal procession down the Mall, Kitty waved from her seat like a queen to her subjects, laughing and smiling all the while. This was the pivotal moment in Kitty's life. It marked the point when she moved, in the blink of an eye, from notoriety to widespread celebrity.

Not everyone was seduced by the quasi-tragic heroine of the hour. One stout yeoman who had witnessed Kitty's escapade shook his walking stick and harrumphed at her infamy: 'Damn my Blood, if this is not too much. Who the Devil would be modest, when they may live in this state by turning [prostitute]. Why, 'tis enough to debauch half the women in London!' This was recounted by another spectator, who wrote a letter which surfaced in the London newspapers. After merrily documenting Kitty's accident, the writer took a moralising tone and labelled Kitty a 'whore'. The public didn't care about Kitty's morals, however. This was merely the beginning wave of a tsunami of 'Fishermania'.[1]

In the following days, the drama garnered column inches. The provincial newspapers drew much of their copy from the London papers, and the story of Kitty's accident spread out to all corners of the country. To Kitty's possible despair, her popularity spawned a series of scurrilous and satirical pamphlets and prints. The idea of a fallen woman falling was irresistible to the Grub Street hacks, and to the eager hordes who read their salacious gossip. Crowds gathered outside print shops' windows, their noses pressed to the glass as they leered at a sketch of Kitty on her back, legs akimbo. Titled 'The Merry Accident', this print asked, 'Who rides fastest, Miss Kitty Fisher or her gay gallant?' It was the lewd humour of the streets and the gutter press. Kitty was presented as a prostitute, as an object of vulgarity and a figure of fun. That cartoonish persona was not, and never was, Kitty. There was always an innocence bordering on naïvety within her. This was part of Kitty's charm and one of the ways that she differed from her fellow courtesans. Nevertheless, the fame heightened her appeal, making Kitty irresistible. Even more men of fashion now vied for the prestige of spending time with the capital's brightest new star. Several wags named their racehorses in her honour. On the turf, gentlemen sniggered at ribald schoolyard innuendo as jockeys 'mounted', 'sat astride', and 'rode' Kitty Fisher.

The publicity was all well and good but Kitty's reputation, both as a high-class courtesan and as an accomplished equestrienne, was under threat. It was embarrassing to have everyone laughing at a scurrilous print in which she lay tumbled on the ground with her skirts up around her waist and her stockings and garter on display. The echoing thread of shame that resonated from her accident was hard to bear. It was to get worse. There was soon a torrent of pamphlets and newspaper articles, some mocking Kitty, some exaggerating her trysts (sex always did sell) and the rest preaching against her immodest lifestyle. If the writers of the latter hoped to make Kitty repent, they failed.

It was now, less than two or three weeks after Kitty's fall, that a pseudo-biography of her life thus far was published, anonymously. *The Juvenile Adventures of Miss K__y F___r*, as a memoir, is a curious mix of fact and fiction. Within its pages, Kitty's real adventures are recounted alongside madcap inventions. There is salacious detail about Kitty's time at the Hammersmith boarding school. The author claimed that every girl there was 'as much debauched in sentiment … as if she had been at a brothel in Covent Garden.' Kitty was not taken out of the school because she was ill, the memoir continued, but because her father worried that she was being preyed upon by men who visited the house.

A tale was gleefully related of how the brother of a schoolgirl, staying the night, managed to peep voyeuristically through a hole in the wainscot into the room Kitty shared with another girl, and watch them pleasuring one another. This same young man laid a plan so he could trap Kitty at a country inn while helpfully escorting her back to Soho for the Whitsun holidays. He made a play for Kitty, which she roundly rebuffed. However, the sexual anecdotes about Kitty's time at school are titillation for the eighteenth-century male reader, put there to spice up the story. Later, Kitty is placed in a French nunnery, a madhouse, and even held overnight in a watch house, apprehended on suspicion of being a prostitute when she was walking home at night.

Due to the wild fictional elements, *The Juvenile Adventures* has been discounted as a credible source for Kitty's life. However, much information can be verified. For instance, although her mother's name is incorrect, the other details of her family and her childhood ring true. The author had got some insight into Kitty's past, and perhaps – despite her protestation – Kitty had collaborated to a degree. It is possible that Kitty and her friend Jane (who was known to be a wit and a satirist), had been duped by the person who wrote it. If so, then the factual elements came from them, and perhaps also some of the mocking, cruel remarks about the men in their lives. Would it be too much of a stretch to think that both women thought the memoir a fun way to capitalise on Kitty's fame? Only to find themselves taken advantage of by the author who slandered their parents and added the sexual elements so titillating to eighteenth-century male readers?

Some of these additions have more than a little in common with the adventures of a contemporary actress, Jane Lessingham. Jane had married a naval man but, while he was at sea, had taken up with an Irishman named Samuel Derrick. He had several strings to his bow. Primarily, Derrick was a writer, the man reputed to have compiled the first edition of *Harris's List*, despite it bearing Jack Harris's name in the title. Another of Derrick's interests was the theatre. One – probably fictional – episode in *The Juvenile Adventures* follows Kitty as she takes acting lessons and tries to make it on the stage. The rival theatre managers David Garrick (of Drury Lane) and John Rich (of Covent Garden) are obliquely referenced. Jane Lessingham had taken lessons from Rich a few years earlier. An added in-joke, if Derrick was the author of *The Juvenile Adventures*, is the inclusion of himself within the text, as Don Livinio. He is described as a dramatic critic and lover of the theatre, labels which fit Samuel Derrick all too well. Don Livinio offered to keep Kitty, and she accepted, according to the memoir. The pimp, Jack Harris (Harrisino), popped up and spread rumours about Kitty in an attempt to get Don Livinio to leave her. An argument ensued between the two men. In real life, Derrick and Harris were rivals, their enmity centred on *Harris's List*. As an experienced hack, and with a personal insight into London's sex industry, Derrick would have no problem in enhancing Kitty's story in print. He is the most probable author, given the clues inside.[2]

The memoir playfully pretends to be set in the Spanish capital but it is quite obvious that it is referencing London. 'In the capital of Spain, the good city of Madrid, there is a quarter which is best rendered in English by the word Soholio. Here lived an honest man called John F_____r, a silver chaser by trade…' Similarly, most of the characters are given a Spanish pseudonym to partially conceal their identity. Anthony George Martin, who had a real Mediterranean heritage, is instantly recognisable. The Military Cupid is given the name Don Cupidino. Many eighteenth-century pamphlets and pseudo-memoirs employed the same tactics, but everyone at the time could easily work out who was being referenced, nevertheless. We are left today to decipher the Georgian era 'in-jokes' contained within their pages. *The Juvenile Adventures* is a prime example of this genre.

It is possible to put real names to the Spanish pseudonyms but, to do so, we must navigate through the fiction to reach the factual evidence. As we have seen, Samuel Derrick was Don Livinio and Jack Harris, Harrisino. Tom Hutchings is named Don Allenzo and a story woven around him. For Kitty, at least, her dealings with Tom were a business transaction, but in the memoir, they are turned into a tragic fairy tale. The author imagined Kitty rescued from an attempted suicide by Don Allenzo's wealthy aunt, who had wanted to adopt Kitty as a child. The aunt took Kitty into her house as a companion and passed her off as a niece. All went well for several months until the servants gossiped about her nephew and Kitty. Returning home unexpectedly, Don Allenzo's aunt found the young couple together, Don Allenzo on his knees at Kitty's feet. Kitty was sent packing. With Don Allenzo professing his love and promising to take care of her, Kitty took rooms in a house off the Haymarket. At this point, the real story begins. Kitty and Don Allenzo, otherwise Hutchings, were lovers and the two were seen, arm-in-arm, at the theatres and Ranelagh. London gossip said that they'd married but Kitty still called herself Catherine Martin. With abrupt coldness, the memoir recounted Hutchings's abandonment of Kitty.

The clues given for Kitty's next two 'keepers', Don Roderigo and the Duke d'Amelo, must have made their identities obvious to any contemporary reader who had a passing acquaintance with high society. They were Sir Charles Bingham and Thomas Bromley, 2nd Baron Montfort, respectively. Don Roderigo found Kitty too expensive, especially after a run of bad luck at the gaming tables. The Duke d'Amelo was described as a young nobleman, just come of age and with more money than sense. Possibly Lord Montfort also had delusions of grandeur, as he is elevated to a ducal coronet when he was just a baron, the lowest peerage. Then there is the Earl of Coventry, called the Count de Peepero. There is no doubt at all about his identification; *The Juvenile Adventures* gleefully recounts the tale of Kitty copying his wife's riding habit. Lord Poulett received a less than flattering representation. His pretended name was Don Gomez and he was described as an old and gouty man. Another contemporary satirical poem, *Kitty's Stream*, contains the lines, 'A fribbling L[or]d the next, worn out, Will have her, spite of age and gout.' This description, of a foolish and frivolous peer, could not be anyone else but Poulett and he must have been incensed to be mocked as elderly, and past his prime.

The wealthy Jewish businessman, Joseph Salvador (a married man), was amongst Kitty's admirers. He had earned a fortune by dealing in precious stones, notably importing diamonds from India. They were always Kitty's favourite jewel and if Salvador gave her a few as a gift, they would have been graciously received. Salvador did provide Kitty with a smart new green vis-à-vis. (A vis-à-vis was a small, narrow carriage in which the two passengers sat facing one another.) Reputedly, the stubborn Kitty once again had Anthony George Martin's cypher painted on its doors, refusing to relinquish Martin's surname. Joseph Salvador is called Don Camelio and noted as the richest of Kitty's lovers.[3]

The Earl of Sandwich appears under the alias of the Count de Slendero. The name poked fun at his appearance, for he was tall and thin (and the European title of count is equivalent to a British earl). Sandwich's lack of a fortune also helps to identify him. He had still been a child when he became an earl and had inherited little money to go with the title. It was well known that he lived frugally. The Count de Slendero was unable to pay Kitty in cash, so gave her his wife's jewels instead. The Countess of Sandwich, increasingly insane, would have been unaware that her jewellery was being dispensed to the capital's courtesans. It is interesting to note that Sandwich's lover, Jane Sumner, mentioned a collection of diamonds in her will. It is likely they had once belonged to the beleaguered countess before finding their way to Jane. Is this evidence that the real-life adventures of Jane and Kitty had become melded together within this pseudo-memoir? Moreover, proof that the two of them collaborated with Derrick in its production? Other men remain unidentified. The fifth member of the gambling club who combined to 'keep' Kitty was the Chevalier de Cumano.

While the first flush of attention had been exhilarating, the baggage that came with it had not been so pleasant. With reluctant acceptance, Kitty had tolerated her defamation in print up to this point. Now, the eponymous heroine of *The Juvenile Adventures* decided she would not brazen it out any longer. Kitty answered her critics. A letter was printed in the *Public Advertiser* newspaper, and there was a good reason for her announcement. Not only had her name been dragged through the mud, but also the names of the men who danced attendance on her. The Earl of Coventry and Joseph Salvador, for instance, both married men, would be angry at having a public light shone onto their private lives. Worse, most of those mentioned had been mocked, and their egos had taken a bashing. Kitty depended on these men financially. The last thing she wanted to do was to alienate them, especially if they suspected that she had a hand in writing the memoir. What might have seemed like fun to a girl not yet out of her teens, whose head had been turned by the sudden attention, now threatened to derail everything. Kitty walked a tightrope; her fame could make or break her and she needed to take control of the situation. Her reply in the *Public Advertiser* said that:

To err, is a blemish intailed upon mortality, and indiscretions seldom or never escape from censure; the more heavy, as the character is more remarkable; and doubled, nay trebled by the world, if the progress of that character is marked by success; then malice shoots against it all her stings, the snakes of envy are let loose; to the humane and generous heart then must the injured appeal, and certain relief will be found in impartial honour. Miss Fisher is forced to sue to that jurisdiction to protect her from the baseness of little scribblers and scurvy malevolence; she has been abused in public papers, exposed in print-shops, and to wind up the whole, some wretches mean, ignorant, and venal, would impose upon the public, by daring to pretend to publish her Memoirs. She hopes to prevent the success of their endeavours, by thus publickly declaring that nothing of that sort has the slightest foundation in truth. C. Fisher.[4]

Kitty's letter was published at the same time as the first volume of *The Juvenile Adventures* was advertised for sale, and well before the second hit the streets a week later. That second volume ended by referencing Kitty's letter to the newspaper and included it in full. The writer of *The Juvenile Adventures* hinted that this was proof that Kitty was all too aware of the publication. The insinuation was that she knew what was going to be written because she had collaborated to a degree. Still, it was a clever ruse, to demonstrably distance herself from the publication, while at the same time pushing it and herself further into the spotlight. Perhaps, though, it was too clever?

Kitty was now famous whether she liked it or not, her celebrity widespread. Gossip about Kitty's antics reached the drawings rooms, coffee houses and taverns of every town in the land. Rumours grew and took on a life of their own and the tale of how she was kept by the men of a gambling club was repeated *ad infinitum*. Kitty played along with her infamy for a time, causing even more of a stir. 'Ladies of the town' such as she were supposed to know their place in society. When it came to visiting the theatre, the side boxes on the lower tiers were considered the best. Positioned as they were, angled towards the stage, they gave more than just a good view of the play. These boxes also allowed the occupants to be seen – and admired – by the crowd sat in the pit and by those in the galleries. They were richly decorated and the preserve of the elite. A courtesan would be expected to sit elsewhere, in a box not so prominently placed.

One evening, either in late March or early April, Kitty stepped out of one of the coaches lining up under the portico at the Theatre Royal on Covent Garden's Drury Lane. She walked into the lobby, ignoring the hubbub her appearance caused. Full of confidence, Kitty breezed into one of the best boxes and settled down, smoothing her wide hooped skirt with a rustle of the finest Spitalfields silk and expensive lace. She turned her face to the stage but knew all eyes were upon her. Her new gown was in the latest fashion and her jewellery reassuringly expensive. The Duchess of Grafton was also at the play that night. She headed for her usual box but, when she walked in, was astonished to come face-to-face with London's newest sensation.

The duchess's husband was the man rumoured to be the Countess of Coventry's lover. The last thing she wanted was women like Kitty sitting in what was the preserve of the elite, tempting errant husbands into further indiscretions. With scant ceremony, the duchess ordered Kitty to leave. Her tone was haughty; she was used to being obeyed. The audience watched agog. The side-show playing out in the box was more interesting than any action on stage could be. Kitty kept her cool and won the day. She politely refused to move and the duchess had no option but to grit her teeth and sit alongside Kitty. Afterwards, Lady Grafton complained loudly about having to do so, and she was determined that Kitty should learn her place. It was reminiscent of Kitty's spat with the Countess of Coventry over the riding habit.

While Kitty was not yet on an equal footing with the women of the aristocracy, she had gained more command when it came to fractious encounters with them.

The Theatre Royal's manager was the former actor, David Garrick. He visited Kitty the next day to ask if she wouldn't mind sitting in a lesser seat on her next visit. The Duchess of Grafton was not the only person who had complained about Kitty's presence in the boxes reserved for ladies and gentlemen of quality. The issue was not just one of social hierarchy. None of those ladies wanted Kitty anywhere near their menfolk and pressure had been put on Garrick to rectify the situation. Kitty was reported to have told him that she was surprised the ladies concerned had objected to being in her company, 'for tho' she had not the honour to know them, she was perfectly acquainted with their husbands.' Garrick left the matter there. Truth be told, all publicity was good and if people came to his theatre to watch the action unfold in the boxes as much as on the stage, he was unlikely to object. Kitty didn't let the furore deter her, either. She doubled down and started a fashion of having tea brought to her, in her box at the opera and theatre. Once Kitty and Jane had tried to copy Elizabeth Chudleigh, Lady Fitzroy, and the Pollard Ashe. Now, where Kitty led, others soon followed. Elizabeth Chudleigh and her coterie caused a fuss when, in the autumn, they visited Covent Garden's theatre every night to watch *The Beggar's Opera*. They 'drank tea in their box, making such a noise and disturbing both the performers and the audience…'[5]

The only man who was not deterred by being named within the pages of *The Juvenile Adventures* was Lord Poulett. The downside for him was that, possibly, the other men of the gambling club had been frightened off by the public scrutiny. Their reputations were of prime importance, whether as married men or as men seeking an heiress to rescue their dwindling fortunes. While their dealings had been conducted with an element of privacy, everything had been fine. Now a light had been shone onto their proceedings and they shied away from becoming embroiled in any further public scandal. Kitty's reputation was of little importance, as far as they were concerned, in contrast to their own.

Poulett was less fazed by how the world at large viewed him. He had no one to answer to. The only problem Lord Poulett had was that, as far as Kitty was concerned, he still wanted to have his cake and eat it. His disreputable friends' agreement to allow Kitty 5 per cent of their winnings had been withdrawn. To Poulett's consternation, he now found himself, to all intents and purposes, Kitty's sole protector and facing the prospect of losing a small fortune in keeping her. The earl didn't intend to do that. Instead, he came up with another plan. It would suit him better to have Kitty hidden away in the country, his and his alone. If he could contrive that, then Poulett wouldn't have to shower Kitty with riches to gain her attention. To the money-conscious earl, this was a big consideration. Kitty wouldn't have turned up her nose at this arrangement if it was going to lead to something more permanent. Even more so if the other men who had collectively kept her had developed cold feet, following the intense scrutiny into her life. It would bring a much-needed level of security into Kitty's world. Perhaps Lord Poulett also suggested that Kitty could escape public censure if she spent time at his Somerset estate? She could lie low and let the fuss calm down.

However, there was one thing missing in this elaborate scheming. While Kitty would happily give up her London life for love, as future events would prove, she had no such feelings where Lord Poulett was concerned. Marriage and a title, however, would compensate for a lack of romance. Kitty hinted to the earl that, if he proposed, she would accept. The earl obfuscated, allowing Kitty to think that he might just be prepared to do that. To become Catherine, Countess Poulett and mistress of a large country estate would fulfil most of Kitty's wishes. It would place her on an equal footing with Maria, Countess of Coventry. The Duchess of Grafton would no longer be able to complain about her presence in the theatre. Kitty would have an entry to society balls and gatherings hitherto denied to her and if she bore the earl an heir, then Kitty's position would be cemented. He was also not in the best of health, and Kitty might soon be left a rich, and titled, widow. She scented a catch. When Poulett invited her down to Somerset, to spend Easter at Hinton St George, Kitty accepted with alacrity.

Hinton St George was then – and still is now – a small hilltop village. The old medieval manor which comprised Hinton House had been added to over the centuries and was a stately hodgepodge of a building when Kitty visited. Encompassing the house was a pleasure garden and parkland with wide-ranging vistas. A banqueting house sat within an artificial 'wilderness' by the bowling green. Lord Poulett had inherited the estate almost sixteen years earlier and was improving his old-fashioned and sprawling manor house. During his tenure, two detached wings were joined to the main house. Possibly, while Kitty visited, building works were ongoing. Even so, it was impressive, and Kitty must have been delighted with the prospect of a countess's coronet and becoming the mistress of Hinton House.[6]

While Kitty was in Somerset angling for a proposal and the chance to become a countess, everyone else in her circle was making for Newmarket in Suffolk, where the races were being held. Newmarket was one of the biggest social gatherings of the year; the king's youngest son, Prince William, Duke of Cumberland, was there for the duration. However, missing Newmarket was of no matter to Kitty if her gouty old earl could be persuaded to offer marriage. Charles Jenkinson (later the 1st Earl of Liverpool) wrote to his friend, the MP George Grenville, speculating on whether Kitty had gone into the country as a wife or as a mistress. Kitty might not have been at Newmarket, but she was the talk of the races. She was also the topic of conversation in a letter sent from the bluestocking Elizabeth Montagu to her friend, Mrs Carter. Mrs Montagu had got her earls mixed up, however, suggesting Kitty had proposed marriage to the Earl of Pembroke.[7]

While everyone else's eyes were fixed on Newmarket, Kitty left Somerset and slipped back into London. She didn't return as a countess but did have an important appointment to keep. She had her first sitting with Joshua Reynolds. He was to paint her portrait, and it would be the first of many. There are several paintings and sketches which are thought to be portraits of Kitty by Reynolds. She became something of a muse to the artist and – if the rumour is to be believed – his lover too, for a while.

The man who is thought to have introduced Joshua Reynolds to Kitty was Augustus Keppel, later the 1st Viscount Keppel. He was the younger son of an aristocratic family and was in his mid-30s. His father was the Earl of Albermarle and, through his mother, Keppel was related to the Duke of Richmond. At just 10 years of age, Keppel entered the navy and that was his career thereafter. He navigated his way through shipwrecks and battles and was once taken as a prisoner-of-war by the French. By the time he made Kitty's acquaintance, Augustus Keppel was a naval hero. A decade earlier, he had been introduced to Joshua Reynolds, then an up-and-coming artist who painted Keppel's portrait and travelled with him on board his ship to the Mediterranean. There Reynolds stayed for two years, studying the Old Masters in Italy and honing his talent. When Kitty sat for him, Reynolds was living – and painting – at his home on the north side of Great Newport Street. Kitty was to pay many visits to that studio, along with the crème-de-la-crème of society. However, if Keppel did make the introduction between Reynolds and the woman he would paint so often during the next few years, it must have been well before Kitty travelled into Somerset. Keppel was on board his ship and in the thick of naval action from the spring of 1759 and remained so throughout the year.[8]

In appearance, Joshua Reynolds was often unkempt. He was shorter than average height, but still head and shoulders above the petite Kitty, and had a florid complexion and lively persona. The West Country burr of his original Devon accent could still be heard in Reynolds's voice. A busy man, he hurried around his studio and was a workaholic, often seeing clients and booking sittings seven days a week. Lady Burlington, described how Reynolds:

> took quite a quantity of exercise while he painted, for he continually walked backward and forward. His plan was to walk away several feet, then take a long look at me and the picture as we stood side by side, then rush up to the portrait and dash at it in a kind of fury. I sometimes thought he would make a mistake, and paint on me instead of the picture. He was very deaf. No, I did not care much for him; he was a very pompous little man.[9]

Kitty's portrait had more significance than might have first been realised. In the end, Lord Poulett decided against proposing marriage to Kitty. Elizabeth Montagu cattily remarked that Earl Poulett's 'family love forms, so perhaps the fair one thought he would approve the legal form of cohabitation; but he hesitated, and so the agreement is made for life, a £1,000 per annum, and a £1,000 for present decorations.' There is nothing other than Mrs Montagu's gossip to suggest that the normally frugal earl settled that amount of money on Kitty. Tongues still wagged across London saying that Kitty was kept by several men, all members of the private gambling club. However, this was no longer the case. Her sudden celebrity status had been a double-edged sword indeed. Sir Charles Bingham and Lord Montfort distanced themselves from her. The Earl of Coventry had been beset on all sides; since the debacle over his wife's riding habit, the countess had insisted on separate beds. She only relented when the earl gave up Kitty. The last man standing had been Earl Poulett and once he realised he was the only one of the disreputable gang left, that too had come to an end. Any hopes Kitty had entertained of an offer of marriage from her earl were dashed.

New men appeared in her life, though, all eager to be admitted to Kitty's presence. Reynolds, once introduced to her, understood what a sensation Kitty's portrait would cause. He knew engravings and prints of this painting would be in high demand and printmaking was a lucrative business at the time. The general public would clamour to own something so intimately connected with Kitty. Those who had no chance of ever affording to buy a portrait of her could still have Kitty's image in their home. The fashion at the time was for 'print rooms'. Engraved prints of royalty, actors, aristocrats and courtesans would be pasted onto the wall, and frames set around them. It is unknown what advantages, financial or otherwise, Reynolds derived from the prints of his portraits. It has been suggested that, as many of his portraits of Kitty were not commissioned, he knew he could gain from the enterprise and painted her with one eye on the print market. For Kitty, too, there may have been a financial benefit but the main one to her was taking control of her public image. Reynolds's portrait of her would almost be an advertisement in her search for a new protector. It would distance Kitty from the sketch of her falling from her horse, and present her as she wished to be seen, a lady of fashion and taste, with a hint of sex appeal.[10]

Between April and June, Kitty sat for Reynolds sixteen times and most of these were early morning appointments, either 8.30 or 9.00 am. Does this signify that Kitty had spent the night with Reynolds, ahead of her sitting first thing the next day? Might the rumours of a romance between artist and muse be true? A writer several years later certainly thought so. In 1769, Joshua Reynolds received a knighthood. Someone calling themselves Fresnoy (believed to be the English painter, the Reverend James Wills) wrote to the *Middlesex Journal*, asking whether Reynolds had not exchanged his honour for the title. He went on to say that 'Catherine has sate [sic] to you in the most graceful, the most natural attitudes; and indeed I must do you the justice to say you have come as near the original as possible.' The implication of his words was clear; he was suggesting that Reynolds had been very close indeed to Kitty. Reynolds himself once confessed that every woman he had ever liked had, in time, grown indifferent to him. Ultimately, his work came first, and Kitty was never one to settle for second-best.[11]

The portrait that resulted from Kitty's first visits to Reynolds's studio was certainly no second-best painting, however. It is considered one of the artist's masterpieces. Kitty sits with a love letter in front of her. It is folded over, and Kitty appears careless of it. No writing is visible except the introduction and date: '*1759, June 2, My Dearest Kit*.' Contemporary engravings have '*My Dearest Life*' instead, and the date may mark the completion of the portrait. Kitty is depicted as an object of desire, a commodity, and as a woman of some independence, each in juxtaposition to the other. She stares directly forward, her head tilted to one side, with something of the coquette in her attitude. Four strands of pearls surround Kitty's neck and ornate earrings hang from her lobes. Her gown is an expensive confection of brown/black silk with tiered lace on the sleeves and ruffles of green ribbon decorating the bodice. She is painted as a society lady, not as a courtesan of growing notoriety and, at first glance, Kitty appears self-assured. James Northcote, Reynolds's pupil, described how his master was able 'to paint his female sitters as "ladies," whether or not they were'. However, Kitty's arms are folded and she sits behind a table, two impenetrable barriers separating her from the viewer. The impression is of someone who is both public and private at the same time, which was, of course, the real conundrum at the heart of Kitty's character. The pose would be replicated by Reynolds in other portraits of aristocratic women as well as those who were, like Kitty, courtesans and mistresses. Other artists followed where Reynolds and Kitty led. The Scottish painter Allan Ramsay depicted several of his sitters in the same attitude, leant on a table, arms folded, and with an expression of knowing confidence.[12]

In no time at all, at least four engravers had copied the portrait and Kitty's likeness was to be had at every print shop in the country. In the windows of these shops, prints of actresses and courtesans competed against those of duchesses and even royalty. They were the eighteenth-century equivalent of today's paparazzi photos. There were even watch-paper prints, designed to fit in the inner lid of a pocket watch, so a gentleman could carry Kitty with him at all times, and sneak a look whenever he wanted. Reynolds, at the beginning of his long and illustrious career, knew that the popularity of these prints raised not only Kitty's profile but also his own. It was – on Reynolds's part at least – a shrewd business move to allow mezzotint engravings of the portrait to be made and circulated as widely as possible.

As for Kitty, while she was now, to all effects and purposes, public property, at least she had retained control over her persona. The engraving of Reynolds's portrait was a vast improvement on the satirical print which showed her sprawled on the ground, after her tumble in the Mall. Now, Kitty was presented as she wished to be seen and remembered. Giustiniana Wynne noted Kitty's rampant celebrity. In the same letter in which she recorded Kitty's *contretemps* with the Countess of Coventry, Guistiniana added that Kitty lived 'in the greatest possible splendour, spends twelve thousand a year, and she is the first of her social class to employ liveried servants – she even has liveried chaise porters. There are prints of her everywhere. She is small and I don't find her beautiful, but the English do and that is what matters.'

In falling from her horse, Kitty had unwittingly eclipsed all her rivals. She had become London's first and foremost celebrity and was at the absolute zenith of her fame. The notoriety brought attendant dangers, though. On a balmy June evening, when the day was about at its longest, Maria, Countess of Coventry was walking in St James's Park with her friend, Lady Waldegrave. The latter was Maria Walpole, and it was just over a month since she had married Earl Waldegrave. The two Marias both wore wide-brimmed hats to give shade from the sun and, with their faces hidden, people began to gossip that it was two 'ladies of the town' who were promenading. Then, someone mistook Lady Coventry for Kitty. The false rumour spread and soon a mob had gathered outside the park. Some wanted to catch a glimpse of the famous Kitty Fisher but others were outraged that public decency was being flouted. 'How dare such women flaunt themselves?' asked the puritans in the mob of each other, working themselves up into a frenzy. They rushed into the park and gave chase, shouting insults. The two countesses were terrified. They began to run and believed they were 'put in great danger of their lives.' Some nearby gentlemen rushed over to help and took hold of one man, Joseph Vivian, who was delivered to the magistrates. The next day, Vivan's abject apology was printed in the newspapers. The king ordered that guards should be placed in London's parks, for the safety of the ladies who visited. Horace Walpole composed a wicked little song about the incident for the entertainment of his friends. He intended it should be sung to the tune of a melody popular at the time, 'Kitty Fisher's Jig':

> I sing not of wars or invasions,
> I tell you a merrier tale –
> How Fisher and Covey were met, Sir,
> And sent all the people to gaol.
> The one was a modest-faced sinner,
> The other a quality toast.
> But Covey could not bear a rival;
> She thought it a terrible case
> That first they should gaze at Kate Fisher,
> And then come and stare in her face.
> 'Indeed, if I were but Moll Gunning,
> They might have done just as they chose;
> But now I am married to Covey,
> They shall not thus tread on my toes.'
> 'I'll make my case known to the King,
> The Monarch I know he adores me,
> And won't suffer any such thing.'
> Then straightaway to Court she betakes her: –
> 'I'm come, Sir, to make my complaint;

I can't walk the park for your subjects,
They stare without any restraint.'
'Shut, shut up the park, I beseech you;
Lay a tax upon staring so hard;
Or, if you're afraid to do that, Sir,
I'm sure you will grant me a guard!'
The boon thus requested was granted:
The warriors were drawn up with care: –
'With my slaves and my guards I'm surrounded,
Come, stare at me now, if you dare!'[13]

Kitty refused to be cowed by Lady Coventry and Lady Waldegrave's ordeal and appeared in state at London's parks and gardens, dressed like royalty and leaning on the arm of a handsome admirer. Keen to capitalise on Kitty's fame, Reynolds persuaded Kitty to sit for a second painting. It was to be a portrait that mocked his contemporary, William Hogarth. The two artists were rivals, both vying for the same patrons. Sir Richard Grosvenor had commissioned Hogarth to execute a painting that he intended would hang in his home. Perhaps unwisely, Sir Richard airily told the artist to choose the subject and to name his price once finished. He anticipated receiving one of Hogarth's wonderful caricature or genre paintings, which the artist painted to great acclaim. However, Hogarth had other ideas for this commission. He was vocal as he painted, trumpeting snippets of news about his progress, perhaps in an attempt to claw attention away from Reynolds. Rather than paint to Sir Richard's expectations, Hogarth took the opportunity to produce a work that – he hoped – would establish him as a painter of dramatic historical subjects. Hogarth drew his inspiration from a medieval short story by an Italian author and painted its heroine, Sigismunda. He used his wife as the model and believed the oil painting would be acclaimed as a masterpiece. It was titled, *Sigismunda Mourning over the Heart of Guiscardo, her murder'd Husband*. In Hogarth's painting, Guiscardo's heart was deposited in a goblet, somewhat gruesomely held in Sigismunda's hand.

Sir Richard Grosvenor was horrified when he was presented with this painting, executed in the style of the Italian Old Masters and so unlike the Hogarthian picture he had wanted. He refused to honour the bargain they had struck and told Hogarth to offer the picture to someone else. Although the painting received favourable reviews when it was exhibited, Hogarth had been humiliated by Sir Richard's refusal to accept the painting. Joshua Reynolds took a keen interest in his rival's discomfort. He began a painting in a similar vein to Hogarth's *Sigismunda* but, for his subject, Reynolds chose to depict the Egyptian queen, Cleopatra. At a sumptuous dinner with her lover, the Roman general Mark Antony, Cleopatra was said to have dissolved a priceless pearl in vinegar (or wine) to win a bet that she could host the most expensive banquet in history. Cleopatra finished this exhibition of her extravagance by drinking the liquid, pearl and all.

While in Italy several years earlier, Reynolds had viewed Francesco Trevisani's *Banquet of Anthony and Cleopatra*. He must have sketched the portrait, for Reynolds's painting of Kitty is a partial copy. It is also reminiscent of a late seventeenth-century portrait by Benedetto Gennari in which Lady Elizabeth 'Betty' Felton adopts the same guise and a similar pose. Betty Felton was as notorious in her day as Kitty was in hers and the painting might have been made for Charles II's illegitimate son, the Duke of Monmouth, who was Betty's lover. A few weeks before Reynolds began his portrait, William Shakespeare's play, *Antony and Cleopatra*, had been performed at the Drury Lane Theatre. David Garrick had played Antony, and Mrs Mary Ann Yates was the Egyptian queen. The performance had been scheduled as *Henry VIII* but the Prince of Wales asked for *Antony and Cleopatra* and so, by royal command, the play was changed. Reynolds decided to capitalise on the current fascination.[14]

For Joshua Reynolds, there was no one more suited to adopt the persona of Cleopatra than Kitty Fisher, a woman who was as noted as the queen for her love of fine jewels. Moreover, Kitty had only recently been kept by the small clique of gamesters, and this may also be alluded to in the subject of the painting. Reynolds painted Kitty as the 'Harlot Queen', holding the pearl above a goblet and about to drop it into the liquid, to win the bet. Copying Betty Felton's portrait, Kitty holds the pearl between her forefinger and thumb in such a way that her fingers make an 'o', which may well have sexual connotations. The pearl is the sitter's 'jewel' which Kitty, like Betty Felton before her, is in full possession of, and can dispose of as she wishes. In her portrait, Kitty wears a white dress, low cut and with blue trimming on the sleeves, richly decorated with pearls. A matching blue wrap falls across one shoulder, together with a ribbon of the same hue that loosely ties back Kitty's chestnut hair, strands of which escape. An ornament – possibly a tiara – is perched upon her head. However, X-ray photography has shown that, originally, Kitty wore a headscarf, which was overpainted. The portrait was in direct competition with Hogarth's *Sigismunda* and was much more popular. Six more sittings in 1759 are recorded for Kitty at Reynolds's studio, spanning the remainder of the year.[15]

Sir Charles Bingham may have commissioned the Cleopatra portrait. He certainly intended to own it, making a down payment of 10 guineas. Once completed, Kitty herself was rumoured to have taken possession of the painting for a short time, although that might have been a clever marketing ploy. Like the first portrait, the *Cleopatra* was engraved and mezzotint prints sold far and wide. These were advertised as being 'done from an Original Picture in [Kitty's] own Possession, lately painted from the Life'. A wag wrote underneath his copy, 'To this fam'd character, how just thy right, / Thy mind as wanton, and thy form as bright.' There is one marked contrast between the printed copies and the original, and that is Kitty's hair which, in the engraving, is neater and the tiara is bigger, more resembling a crown. In what was, probably, a shrewd and calculated business move, Reynolds did not exhibit this portrait. If the general public wanted to marvel at Kitty Fisher as Cleopatra, then they had to buy a print. Knowing that the original not only depicted the famous courtesan but was owned by her as well increased the popularity of those prints, if not the actual portrait. Once Kitty had returned it to Reynolds, and despite later payments from Bingham (who, it seems, never quite got over Kitty), the portrait remained with the artist for over fifteen years. It was purchased in 1776 by Reynolds's friend, the art collector, John Parker, 1st Baron Boringdon. Parker had a significant connection with Kitty Fisher: his mother, Catherine, was the sister of Kitty's Earl Poulett. Parker took the painting back to his home, Saltram House in Devon, and there it remained for more than a century.[16]

A writer signing himself as Crito heard the gossip about the portrait while it was being painted. His letter was published in the *London Chronicle*:

> The charming Kitty now vies in splendor with Cleopatra herself. Whether she rolls in her stately carriages, swings in her superb sedan, or ambles on her pye-bald nag, the trappings of luxury which decorate the fair, proclaim the triumphs of her charms, the munificence of her admirers, and the opulence of this prosperous nation.
>
> Kitty is the theme of every tongue, and the wish of every heart. The slaves of beauty bow down before her, while staffed courtiers, who carry wands without being Conjurers, are ensnared within the magic of her circle. Lords forget their titles, and aim at no higher honours than to be her votaries. Warriors throw aside their truncheons to toy with Kitty. Even old Triton was ambitious to board so rich a prize; but, alas! the envious Morpheus snatched him from the unequal conflict...[17]

'Old Triton' may be a salacious reference to George Anson, 1st Baron Anson. At 62 years of age, Anson had enjoyed a long and distinguished naval career. He was rumoured to be among Kitty's consorts. However, he is also remembered as being devoted to his wife, Elizabeth. She was almost three decades younger than her husband, a woman ahead of her times and noted as a political correspondent. Their only known marital woe was that they had no children. Baroness Anson died in the summer of 1760. Possibly her husband paid some clumsy compliment to Kitty before that, but he was no lothario. A quiet, shy, and stolid man, he took scant notice of the fashionable world. Gossip, however, suggested otherwise. Anson is more than likely the 'naval wight' mentioned in yet another attack on Kitty in verse. *Kitty's Stream: or, the Noblemen turned Fisher-men, a Comic Satire addressed to the Gentlemen in the Interest of the Celebrated Miss K___y F____r* was written at a crucial point in the Seven Years' War. France was planning to invade Britain, although British naval victories later in the year put paid to the attempt. However, the writer of *Kitty's Stream* was not to know that. He lamented the fact that the country's military and naval heroes, peers and strategists were all dancing attendance on Kitty. They were, he said, ignoring the crisis to instead revel in a harlot's arms, and putting the whole country in danger by doing so. The verse was reissued under a different title, *The Adventures of the Celebrated Miss Kitty F____r, or, Who will Fish in a Silver Stream with an hundred Pound Bait*. The title played on the fact that Kitty was reputed to charge £100 a night. This version of the satirical verse stated on the front page that 'Little Wh__es oft' submit to Fate, / While great ones do enjoy the World in State.' The allusion to fishing was also referenced by the artist Paul Sandby, who produced a series of drawings, *Twelve London Cries Done From The Life*. One depicts a raggedy, dirty street hawker of ballads and chapbooks who holds a fishing rod. He walks along, calling out, 'Fun upon Fun, or the first and second part of Miss Kitty Fisher's Merry Thought. / No joke like a true joke. / Come, who'll fish in my fishpond?' The pamphlet that Sandby captured the seller hawking, *Kitty Fisher's Merry Thought; or, No Joke like a True Joke* contained a full-length print of Kitty. Her pseudonym had overtaken her and her nickname was on everyone's lips. It seemed impossible that Kitty Fisher would ever escape her celebrity.[18]

Perhaps it was while travelling back and forth to Reynolds's studio that Kitty had attracted the attention of two of the royal princes. George, Prince of Wales was a few days shy of his twenty-first birthday, and heir to the throne (his father, Frederick, Prince of Wales, had died some years earlier). With him was his youngest brother, Prince Frederick, just nine years old. He pointed Kitty out to his elder brother and the Prince of Wales was surprised that Frederick had recognised Kitty. He asked the youngster if he knew who she was. 'Why, a Miss,' replied Frederick. 'A Miss,' said the Prince of Wales, 'why, are not all girls Misses?' Frederick, with a comical air of gravity given his age, confided to his elder brother that Kitty was a 'particular sort of Miss, a Miss that sells oranges.' However, he went on, 'they are not such oranges as you buy – I believe they are a sort that my brother Edward buys.'

His Royal Highness, Prince Edward (later the Duke of York and Albany) was close in age to the Prince of Wales. Just under ten months separated the two brothers but they were as different as could be. Where George was serious and sensible, Edward was giddy and frivolous. The lure of royalty was irresistible to Kitty. She is said to have been introduced to Prince Edward and that afterwards he visited her house and spent the night there. In the morning, Edward gave Kitty £50, half what she was rumoured to charge for a night's entertainment. Keen to repeat the experience, Edward visited Kitty again a few evenings later. Once more, he spent the night in Kitty's bed. This time, however, he asked Kitty to accept just £20, saying it was all he had. Royalty or not, Kitty knew her worth. She was not going to sell herself short to any man, prince, peer, or commoner. Kitty gave orders to her servants that Prince Edward should not be admitted again.[19]

Kitty counted high-ranking military officers as well as naval within her circle of new admirers. John, Viscount Ligonier (later the 1st Earl Ligonier), an elderly French-born general in the king's army, also paid court to her. Ligonier was the son of a Huguenot family. They had fled from France after the Edict of Nantes, which had protected the rights of Huguenots in the country for almost a century, was revoked in 1685. Just like Kitty's father, Ligonier ended up in England. He joined the army, and his bravery led to speedy promotion through the ranks. Royal approval helped too. Not only was Ligonier on good terms with George II, but also, unusually, with the heir, Frederick, Prince of Wales. The king and his eldest son (while he lived) were at loggerheads and most courtiers fell into one camp or the other. That he maintained a good relationship with both was a testament to Ligonier's innate diplomacy. In 1757, he was rewarded with the appointment of Commander-in-Chief of the British armed forces.

When he met Kitty, Ligonier was in his late seventies and had never married. Several women, actresses and opera singers, had been linked to him over the decades and his reputation was that of a lover as much as a hero. The *Town and Country Magazine*, writing just after the death of Ligonier in 1770, claimed that, like the Earl of Sandwich, the viscount often made a merry trio with Kitty and her friend, Jane Sumner. However, the author of the piece suggested that Ligonier was only dancing attendance on Kitty because it was fashionable to do so. He declared that 'a *debauchee*, upon the *bon ton*, considers it as great a disgrace, not to have had an alliance with the prevailing *Thaïs*, as he would to wear a *Kivenhuller* hat when the *Nivernois* are so much in vogue.' With an increasing note of darkness, the same article hinted that Ligonier preferred younger girls. Kitty, at the time, was still in her late teens.[20]

Kitty now came to the notice of the king, although she didn't get to meet him personally. George II was conducting a review of the troops in Hyde Park. A huge crowd gathered to watch and amongst them was Kitty Fisher. She attracted as much, if not more, attention as the royal party and the soldiers marching back and forth. The king was surrounded by a clique of courtiers, including John, Viscount Ligonier. He was at George II's side when somebody suggested they play a prank on 'the Great Commoner', William Pitt. The nickname was given because, up to that point, Pitt had repeatedly refused to accept a title although later he was created 1st Earl of Chatham. At the time, he was Secretary of State for the Southern Department, a cabinet position that was a forerunner of the Home Office. Pitt's jurisdiction covered southern England, Wales, and Ireland as well as the American colonies and any European country which was predominantly Catholic or Muslim in faith. The courtiers spotted Kitty and pointed her out to the king, who asked what her name was. Ligonier replied, 'Oh, sir, it is the Duchess of N___, a foreign lady, whom the Secretary should know.' As the courtiers had anticipated, the king declared that Mr Pitt ought to be introduced to this intriguing foreign duchess.

Ligonier was despatched to lead Pitt to Kitty while the courtiers watched, sniggering behind their hands. He performed the introductions with studied courtesy, 'This is Mr Secretary Pitt – Miss Kitty Fisher.' The intention was to embarrass Pitt, but the joke fell flat. He neither recoiled from being in the company of such a notorious woman nor became tongue-tied and bashful. Instead, without missing a beat, the Secretary of State swept a deep bow in front of Kitty. He told her he was sorry he'd not had the honour of knowing her when he was younger. 'For then, Madam,' Pitt said, 'I should have had the hope of succeeding in your affections, but old and infirm as you now see me, I have no other way of avoiding the force of such beauty but by flying from it.' (Pitt was around 50.) With that, he bid Kitty good day and strolled away and a few of the king's companions came over to Kitty, laughing. They assumed she had made fun of Pitt and sent him away with his tail between his legs, but Kitty put them right. 'Not I, indeed,' Kitty told them. 'He went off of his own accord, to my very great regret, for I never had such handsome things said of me by the youngest man I ever was acquainted with.'[21]

That was the real problem for Kitty. The young men who were in thrall to her wanted her body and the éclat of being in her company. What they didn't want was to marry the infamous Kitty Fisher, preferring to settle down with a lady their equal or better in both rank and fortune. In the end, while Maria Walpole and the Gunning sisters became countesses, and even duchesses, Kitty became neither. A few lines in the contemporary press may refer to her disappointment. 'The Report given out, that a celebrated Courtezan was soon to be married to a Person of Distinction, is without Foundation, that Gentleman only wanting her as the little Mistress of an Hour.' Earl Poulett faded from Kitty's life. He died, still a bachelor, five years later. Despite everything, Kitty was still in need of a new keeper.[22]

Chapter Five

Bonnets, Banknotes, and Brushstrokes

'You, Madam, are become the Favourite of the Public and the Darling of the Age; you are the Admiration of every Eye, the Theme of every Tongue; your Beauty staggers Resolution, unguards the Wary, and disarms the Strong. Youth sickens with Desire, and Age chuckles at the Sight and feels returning Vigour. Your Lovers are the Great Ones of the Earth, and your Admirers among the Mighty; they never approach you but, like Jove, in a Shower of Gold.'

(*An Odd Letter on a Most Interesting Subject,*
to Miss Kitty Fisher, 1760)

A culture of celebrity had emerged in the eighteenth century. Previous to this, people who had acquired a level of fame had been 'celebrated' but weren't celebrities as we understand the term today. By the middle of the 1700s, that had changed. Gossip from London's coffee houses, pleasure gardens, and clubs echoed around the country, peddled by the increased demand for newspapers and the popularity of prints. Anyone could hear Kitty's name or have her pretty face, as painted by Joshua Reynolds, in their home. A courtesan with the wit to think ahead could maximise her publicity with these prints, and also by forging good relations with the era's press. Several women made particular friends of newspaper hacks, ensuring they had a conduit for releasing stories into the press, and therefore keeping their profile high. It's not so different to someone in the public eye today calling a photographer to capture them taking a pap walk. Kitty's acquaintance with Samuel Derrick was in this vein. She was famous for the scandal that surrounded her life and was known, in short, because she sold her body to men of title and wealth. Kitty's skill was in transcending that and cultivating her image as one of taste and refinement, of fashion and beauty. It set Kitty apart from her counterparts and was the reason she rose to the top, the first ever female celebrity in the modern sense.

Kitty had money, a roof over her head, a fine coach, jewels, and beautiful gowns. She was the talk of London. Life had become an exhilarating, almost unstoppable maelstrom. However, Kitty lacked some important things, elements that were of the utmost importance to her, specifically security and romance. Kitty was caught between two personas, the hard-nosed courtesan and the soft-hearted girl from Soho who craved love. It's easy to forget just how young Kitty still was, not yet out of her teens. For a while, her head was turned, and she believed the hype which surrounded her. Then, in the autumn of 1759, Anthony George Martin's son was christened in Soho. Despite everything which had happened since Kitty and Martin had parted, she must have felt this as a body blow. Shortly afterwards, Kitty's friend Jane Sumner fell pregnant. The father was probably her lover, the Earl of Sandwich. He wanted nothing to do with either the child or his pregnant mistress.

Abandoned by Lord Sandwich, Jane Sumner managed to gain for herself that which was missing in Kitty's life. Jane began a new relationship with the MP William Skrine, formerly of Claverton Manor in Somerset. When Jane's daughter was born, Skrine took on the role of a stepfather. He was a wealthy man (the son of a Bath physician) but, like so many others, he gambled away his evenings. Skrine's father had used his fortune to buy Claverton Manor, a medieval manor house near Bath. In 1758, William Skrine had sold the estate, maybe to cover a debt incurred at cards. As Skrine was a gamester, he may have come to know Jane via the gambling club which had kept her friend, Kitty Fisher. With Jane's belly growing large, the Earl of Sandwich was happy for Skrine to have her. He turned elsewhere for his entertainment and didn't have to look too far.

Kitty must have known that any relationship with Lord Sandwich was just a dalliance, but the truth was that he was the best on offer at that time. The wise course of action was to take what she could in the way of gifts, while they were on the table. Kitty managed to get a promise from the earl that he would buy her a harp. She waited a while, in expectation, but the instrument failed to make an appearance in her rooms. As she had once pestered the Earl of Coventry about the riding habit, Kitty now kept on reminding Lord Sandwich that he owed her a harp. At last, she brought matters to a head by suggesting that they should call the earl's carriage, there and then, and go to buy one. Kitty had caught her peer in a good mood. Perhaps he had just had a win at the tables and felt disposed to be generous? To Kitty's delight, he agreed and they set off to a luthier's shop. She was soon running her fingers over the strings of several harps, ranging in price from 20 to 80 guineas. Kitty's choice was a richly decorated harp. It was also the most expensive. Sandwich argued for the cheapest one, but it was very plain. He refused to listen to Kitty's pleas, saying all the harps sounded the same and that was the most important thing. Not to Kitty, it wasn't. An ornamented harp worth 80 guineas would be an investment and, more than that, it underscored her worth. She refused to let Sandwich buy the cheapest harp. Whirling around, Kitty left the shop, ran to the carriage, and ordered the coachman to take her home. The Earl of Sandwich was left bemused and stranded.[1]

Kitty found other men to spend her time with. She was still seen at the theatre and pleasure gardens. On one occasion, at Ranelagh, such a crowd gathered to watch Kitty drink tea in one of the booths that guards had to be employed to stop her being mobbed. She was always dressed in the latest style. The fashion of the period was for Rococo-influenced gowns, worn over hoops or panniers. Extremely popular was the *robe à la française*, often with what was known as a sack back. This extra fabric at the back of the dress was arranged in two large box pleats which fell from the shoulders to the floor, giving the impression of a train. Evening dresses would be made of silks, day dresses from floral chintz and cottons. The overskirt of the dress opened at the front to display the underskirt and a stomacher covered the laces of the low-cut bodice, under which would be boned stays. Flounces of costly lace, gold fringing, tassels, and embroidery decorated the gown. Once it had been Maria, Countess of Coventry who had set the style. Now, Kitty, with her innate sense of fashion and love of frippery, led and others followed. Despite her infamy, women dressed to imitate her. If Kitty was desirable to men, then they wanted to look just like her. It had ever been so.

A few years earlier, the latest must-have fashion accessory had been the 'Fanny Murray Cap'. It could be found displayed in the windows of every on-trend millinery shop up and down the country. Rather like a cocked hat, the wide brim curved upwards at the front and back. Two ribbons or tassels hung down from one side and the hat was tied with ribbons under the chin and worn at a jaunty angle. It was named after another member of Kitty's impure sisterhood, Frances 'Fanny' Murray.

According to Fanny's memoirs, she was born in Bath during the late 1720s, making her Kitty's senior by just over a decade. The daughter of Thomas Rudman, a musician, Fanny sold posies and nosegays on the steps of Bath's theatre as a child. Then, at just 13 years of age, Fanny was debauched by the 1st Duke of Marlborough's rakehell grandson, Jack Spencer. Despite her youth, she next became the mistress of Bath's Master of Ceremonies. Richard (Beau) Nash, a wealthy tradesman's son turned unofficial 'king' of Bath, was almost four decades Fanny's senior. When that ended and while still in her teens, Fanny wound up in London, living in Covent Garden and calling herself Fanny Murray. She was working in one of London's many brothels until she was mentioned in that infamous 'whore's directory', *Harris's List*. The inclusion fixed Fanny's fame. She was, for a time, the Earl of Sandwich's mistress, before Jane Sumner caught his eye. When Kitty became a courtesan, Fanny was just past 30 and had given up her former occupation.[2]

With Fanny retired from public life, it was left to Kitty to dazzle in her place. By the autumn of 1759, it was the celebrated Kitty Fisher who was recognised by all as the newest style icon. Even the simplest of her gowns were set off with costly jewellery. On 25 October 1759, Lady Caroline Fox wrote to her sister, the Countess of Kildare, to say that:

> I saw a young woman t'other day at Court that pleases me more than any I have seen for years except my own sisters. 'Tis Lady Northampton. She is not a beauty, but so much sense, modesty and air of a woman of fashion both in manner and person make her vastly pleasing. None of the Kitty Fisher style either in dress or manner, which all the young women affect now.[3]

Not to be outdone by Fanny Murray, Kitty also set trends in headgear. As a former milliner, she knew how to create a show-stopping hat, but imitation is the sincerest form of flattery. While there is little left to describe with precision what the 'Kitty Fisher Bonnet' looked like, from the scant evidence available it appears to be a partial copy of the 'Fanny Murray Cap'.

Strange as it may seem, the best idea we can get of Kitty's famous bonnet is from a painting of two girls dressing a kitten by candlelight. The artist was Joseph Wright of Derby, and the picture postdates Kitty's life by a year or two but contains a series of 'in-jokes' relating to Kitty. At first glance, it depicts an innocent scene in which two young girls have put down their doll and begun, as a game, to dress up their pet kitten. However, it has darker undertones. In Dutch art, a cat 'could symbolise danger, luxury, sensuality and lust; when shown with children at play, they engaged themes of discipline and education, seduction and the pains of love.' The kitten, which is a tomcat, has at some point had his genitalia overpainted during the last 250 years, but his tail, protruding between the hind legs, is suggestive of masculine arousal. It has been suggested that both the doll and the kitten (the kitty-cat) refer to Kitty Fisher. An eighteenth-century viewer would have got the joke, made in a 'nudge-nudge (wink-wink)' style. Several clues support this theory. The girls' doll, which lays discarded with its skirt and petticoat awry, is reminiscent of Kitty's fall from her horse, the episode which catapulted her into public notoriety. She is dressed in a pink gown, decorated with lace. Despite the kitten being a tomcat, a 1781 engraving of the painting bore the title 'Miss Kitty Dressing'. Does the bonnet or cap with which the kitten has been dressed give a further clue to the contemporary viewer? Does he wear a Kitty Fisher Bonnet? If so, then the hat appears to have a small lace-edged brim that is curved back on either side, making the front a sweetheart peak. Above this peak are some pink flowers and what may be ribbons. Although it is difficult to see, the brim at the back also appears to curve up, in imitation of the Fanny Murray Cap and similar to a male tricorn. There are more additions to be found in the engraving of the portrait. Along with the ribbons and a sprig of flowers, the bonnet is decorated with two feathers, standing upright. This gives it height, a fact that the petite Kitty would have appreciated. As further proof that this is indeed the famed Kitty Fisher Bonnet, in one of Joseph Reynolds's portraits of her, Kitty wears a dainty cap that looks very similar to the one worn by the kitten.[4]

Reynolds's portrait of Kitty wearing what may be her trademark bonnet was never finished. Had it been then it would, perhaps, have been the most impressive of Reynolds's portraits of Kitty. It is said that this was the painting on Reynolds's easel when he died. Maybe he had returned to the unfinished portrait, determined to complete it at the very end of his life and knowing it would rank as one of his masterpieces? If the painting had been commissioned, then this detail has been lost to time. Nor is the date of its execution known, although it must have been commenced in either 1759 or 1760. In size, it is similar to the first painting in which Kitty is holding the letter. Her pose also mimics that portrait. Formal, but still maintaining a sensual quality, Kitty again sits at a table, her arms folded in front of her, returning the gaze of the viewer. Kitty's head is tilted to the side and her expression is softer but still seductive. She appears to be lost in thought and the portrait as a whole has a dreamlike quality to it. Around Kitty's neck is a simple black band and her only jewels are a pair of pearl drop earrings. Over a gown that appears to be blue is a gauzy wrap that covers – but does not obscure – Kitty's décolletage. No doubt, had the portrait been completed, there would also have been rich lace edging Kitty's sleeves. She is every inch the archetypal society lady, apart from that knowing gaze with which she stares out from the canvas.[5]

Kitty's hair is powdered and fastened tightly back. On top of her head is a neat cap or bonnet. Although the 'sweetheart' line at the front is not pronounced, the headgear worn by Kitty in this portrait does lift at the front on either side. The sprig of flowers and upright feathers of the engraving are missing but there are blue ribbons and flowers placed exactly where the pink ones were on the bonnet worn by Joseph Wright of Derby's little tomcat. There is a suggestion in the painting that the back of the hat is also curved upwards. This, then, would seem to be the bonnet that Kitty wore to such acclaim that women across the world clamoured to own a similar one. Kitty's fame was such that, by 1760, the Kitty Fisher Bonnet was being advertised as far away as Boston in America. It was still remembered twenty years later. At the famous Don Saltero's Coffee House in Chelsea (opened in the late seventeenth century by James Salter and still bearing his pseudonym decades later) were multiple glass cabinets containing 'curiosities'. On a shelf in one of these, alongside such exotic, diverse, and wonderful exhibits as the tusk of an otter, Oliver Cromwell's seal, a couple of locusts, and a Chinese ladies' back scratcher, was 'Miss Kitty Fisher's favourite cap of flowers, made of shells'.

Taking over from Fanny in the fashion stakes was not the only way in which Kitty outdid her forerunner. For many years, Fanny Murray

In this unfinished portrait, by Sir Joshua Reynolds, Kitty appears to be wearing her famous 'Kitty Fisher Bonnet'. (*Elton Hall*)

Above, King Square in Soho (now Soho Square). Kitty was born on King Street which is in the maze of streets to the top right. Below, Covent Garden with its famous market, and equally infamous nightlife, was only a short stroll away from Kitty's childhood home. (*Yale Center for British Art*)

Above, rural Hammersmith where Kitty went to school (*Yale Center for British Art*). Below, two contrasting views of the millinery trade. *(Left, National Museum and right, The Lewis Walpole Library)*

Above left, Sir Joseph Mawbey, the Vauxhall distiller whom Kitty turned down (*Rijksmuseum*) and right, Sir Charles Bingham, 1st Earl Lucan, both in later life (*Yale Center for British Art*). Middle, Thomas Hutchings Medlycott. Below, Thomas Bromley, Lord Montfort. (*The Lewis Walpole Library*)

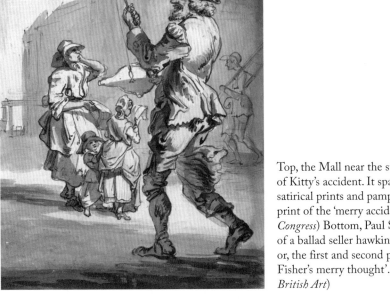

Top, the Mall near the stable yard, the site of Kitty's accident. It spawned a host of satirical prints and pamphlets. Middle, a print of the 'merry accident'. (*Library of Congress*) Bottom, Paul Sandby's depiction of a ballad seller hawking 'Fun upon fun, or, the first and second part of Miss Kitty Fisher's merry thought'. (*Yale Center for British Art*)

Above left, an engraved print of Sir Joshua Reynolds's first portrait of Kitty Fisher. (*Yale Center for British Art*) Above right, King George II; Kitty was pointed out to him at a military revue in Hyde Park. (*Nationalmuseum*) Below, Earl Poulett's ancestral pile, Hinton House, which Kitty visited while hoping for a proposal. (*The History and Antiquities of the County of Somerset*)

Engravings of Kitty Fisher and her contemporaries. Above left, Kitty Fisher in the guise of Cleopatra, above right, Maria, Countess Waldegrave, née Walpole and below left, Nelly O'Brien, all after portraits by Sir Joshua Reynolds. Below right, Lucy Cooper after a portrait by Herman van der Myn. (*Yale Center for British Art*)

Above, Ranelagh Gardens' Rotunda, inside which ladies and gentlemen would promenade. (*Yale Center for British Art*) Below, the Grand Walk in Marylebone Gardens. (*Birmingham Museum and Art Gallery*)

Two views of Vauxhall Gardens, above an overhead view showing the layout and below, the Grand Walk and orchestra. (*Yale Center for British Art*)

The sort of gown that Kitty would have worn. It is made of silk plain weave (faille), patterned with silk and metallic thread, and decorated with metallic lace. Made in England, it dates to c.1765. Under the dress would be a corset and hoop petticoat. (*LACMA*) Kitty was known to use skin-whitening make-up, following the fashions set by Mme Pompadour, amongst others. (*Harvard Art Museums*)

Left, a print showing Joseph Wright of Derby's painting, *Miss Kitty Dressing*. It is thought that the kitten wears a 'Kitty Fisher Bonnet' and that the doll represents Kitty. (*National Gallery of Art*) Below left, Fanny Murray, Kitty's predecessor, wearing her trademark 'Fanny Murray Cap'. (*Herzog August Bibliothek, Wolfenbüttel*) Below right, the Gunning sisters, Elizabeth, Duchess of Hamilton and Kitty's great rival, Maria, Countess of Coventry. (*National Gallery of Ireland*)

Above, the Jacobean house which William Richard Chetwynd expected to inherit, Ingestre Hall, as he would have known it apart from some early nineteenth-century additions by John Nash. (*Yale Center for British Art*) Below, Kitty Fisher in the guise of Danaë, by Sir Joshua Reynolds. It has been described as his most erotic painting. (*Wikimedia Commons*)

Sir Joshua Reynolds (above, left) painted many portraits of Kitty Fisher. (*Metropolitan Museum of Art*) In his portrait of Kitty shown above, right, she is thought to be holding his pet parrot. (*Wikimedia Commons*) Kitty visited Reynolds's house and studio in Leicester Square (below) for many of her sittings; it was one of the houses on the left. (*Yale Center for British Art*)

Above, Kennington Common, where Kitty Fisher's coachman was hanged in retribution for his terrible crime. (*Yale Center for British Art*) The king was horrified that a mob tried to halt the execution. Below, George III and Queen Charlotte in their coronation robes. (*Indianapolis Museum of Art*)

To quell gossip, Kitty and John Norris had to marry for a second time at St George's in Hanover Square, shown above. (*Yale Center for British Art*) Soon after her marriage, Kitty was taken ill. She died in a room at Bath's Three Tuns lodging house. It is the building with the pointed roofs on the right of the image below. (*Wellcome Library*)

There are three known copies of this portrait of Kitty Fisher with doves by Sir Joshua Reynolds, all very similar. The identity of the man shown in the locket around her neck is not known. It may possibly be William Richard Chetwynd. (*New York Public Library*)

was in the keeping of Sir Richard Atkins, who paid through the nose to provide her with every luxury. Despite this, Fanny continued to entertain a constant stream of other men in her bedroom, both low and highborn. Perhaps this was because, on occasion, Atkins was not generous enough? Horace Walpole related the following anecdote in a letter to his friend, George Montagu:

> I liked her [Fanny's] spirit in an instance I heard t'other night; she was complaining of want of money; Sir Richard Atkins immediately gave her a twenty pound note; she said 'Damn your twenty pound, what does that signify!' – clapped it between two pieces of bread and butter and eat [sic] it.[6]

When Giacomo Casanova wrote his *Memoirs*, he recounted this half-remembered story. In his version, though, he exaggerated the value of the banknote and placed Kitty – who had eclipsed Fanny Murray's fame – centre stage. Possibly, Casanova did meet Kitty during his stay in England during the summer of 1763, perhaps on a balmy evening in Vauxhall Gardens. If so, his memory of that occasion was more than a little hazy. Casanova claimed his intimate and equally disreputable friend, the Frenchman, Pierre Angel Goudar, introduced him 'to all the most famous courtezans in London, above all to the illustrious Kitty Fisher, who was just beginning to be fashionable'. Goudar had been in London for two years by that time and was well known to many of the women who worked in the capital's sex trade.

Of course, Kitty's notoriety had begun four years before Casanova visited England. The libertine embellished his story further. He placed Kitty in the house of 'the well-known procuress, Mrs Wells', waiting for a smitten duke to arrive and take her to a ball. Kitty was, Casanova said, dripping with diamonds worth thousands of pounds, but Goudar promised she would be his for five guineas. This was well below the price Kitty set upon herself and so another discrepancy in the lothario's memory of events. Casanova claimed that he approached Kitty and complimented her, using the only English words he knew: 'I love you.' Kitty laughed and began to chatter away, in English. Although other accounts remember that Kitty spoke perfect French, Casanova claimed she could not speak a word of his language. Comparing the sensitivity of his hearing with the sensation of touch, Casanova said he began to feel dizzy. He thought Kitty jabbered like a magpie and, as he liked to enjoy the full range of all his senses, Casanova decided not to take things further. The last accusation is the only one that rings true. Kitty was known as a chatterbox.[7]

While Kitty might well have been tricked out with diamonds, her favourite jewels, it doesn't fit that, in 1763, she would have been present in the house of a known bawd. It was from Mrs Wells that Casanova claimed he heard the tale about Kitty Fisher and a banknote. Kitty had, it was said, swallowed a £100 banknote on a slice of buttered bread. On another occasion, Casanova continued, Mr Pitt's brother-in-law had lit Kitty's bowl of flaming punch with a note of the same amount. The great libertine was not impressed, saying, 'I know nothing more stupid than these boastful remarks; only the owners of the bank can find them in good taste.'

Apocryphal stories, then, and ones with echoes of Cleopatra and the pearl. It was Fanny Murray who was reputed to have eaten the banknote, and the man who Casanova claimed lit Kitty's punch with a banknote is identifiable as Fanny's lover Sir Richard Atkins (his sister Penelope married George Pitt, 1st Baron Rivers). Wonderful as these tall tales are concerning Kitty, they are false. Kitty never made a meal of a banknote, of any denomination, nor had her punch lit with one. However, it is a measure of Kitty's celebrity that stories of Fanny Murray's escapades from years before were retold and attributed to her much younger rival. In turn, these tales have become established as part of Kitty Fisher's myth and legend. After Sir Richard Atkins's early death in 1756 (well before Kitty had gained her iconic status), Fanny had been left at the mercy of her creditors. She was rescued from a sponging house gaol by the son of her debaucher, the upstanding John Spencer, 1st Earl Spencer. In an attempt to right his father's wrongs, Earl Spencer settled £200 a year on an actor named David Ross, on the condition that he married Fanny. When Kitty was famous, Fanny was living a respectable middle-class life as Mrs Ross. She was yesterday's news and Casanova barely mentioned her in his *Memoirs*.[8]

Fanny never learned the wisdom of putting money by for a rainy day. She spent every penny she had earned and, but for her marriage, would have faced destitution. Her life should have been an example to others who followed in her footsteps but Kitty, young and reckless, spent with wild abandon, especially when it was someone else's money. While the story about Kitty eating the banknote has been repeated *ad infinitum* over the intervening centuries, other tales regarding Kitty's love of excess have been forgotten. One concerns a hunt for summer fruit on a cold January day. Kitty decided on a whim that she wanted to eat a bowl of strawberries. Nothing else would satisfy her, and so a search was made. At last, some were found in a gardener's greenhouse. He could only make up a small basket, though, and wanted 30 guineas for doing so. There were about forty strawberries in the basket, and Kitty insisted on having them despite the extortionate price. It is not known which of her lovers paid up. As was pointed out at the time, 30 guineas would have bought a field large enough to grow strawberries for an entire city to eat.[9]

We just don't know whether or not Kitty took any lessons from the fate of women like Fanny Murray. It was said that she used her money to help her family and friends, but did Kitty put some to one side for her future? For about a year, she had been showered with riches before, with surprising suddenness, Kitty turned her back on the glare of self-publicity. During the summer of 1760, Kitty visited Bath, but her presence garnered barely any attention. Her notoriety had been built on flimsy ground. Even at the height of her fame, Kitty's private life was conducted mostly behind closed doors. Other than the fall from her horse, she behaved with decorum and did very little in the public eye that would cause censure. Although, as the furore at the theatre showed, her very presence could sometimes be enough to provoke a scandal.

Kitty herself started to vanish from sight, although her name remained a byword for immorality. While she had slipped out of the public's gaze, songs, verses, and pamphlets all continued to mention the famous Kitty Fisher. A collection of bawdy poems (together with a sermon by two Methodists for good measure) had nothing to do with Kitty other than its title, *Miss Kitty F--h-r's Miscellany*, and a dedication to her by the unnamed author. There was also an 'it narrative' that was peddled to eager readers. This kind of story was popular at the time and followed the adventures of an object or animal. *Chrysal, or, the Adventures of a Guinea* was told from the perspective of a coin as it passed through various hands. A young man handed it over as payment after a visit to a courtesan. The woman was not named but, from the details given, it was obvious that it was meant to depict Kitty. Another publication, *An Odd Letter on a Most Interesting Subject to Miss Kitty Fisher*, by an author naming himself Simon Trusty, berated Kitty on her lack of maternal instincts. By the use of contraception, the writer of this cruel, moralising pamphlet claimed, Kitty was behaving unnaturally in depriving herself of motherhood. Simon Trusty was, perhaps, a little out of touch with Kitty's life when he wrote his piece, however. While she never became a mother, Kitty's life had taken a dramatic turn.

The only record of Kitty's visit to Bath that year is to be found in what, at first glance, appears to be a sarcastic little poem. The introductory details to this rhyme are, however, oddly specific. They are detailed enough to make one believe that the sighting of Kitty, which led to the verse being written, was genuine. In the eighteenth century, high society followed a 'season'. While parliament was sitting, from October till June, the upper classes spent most of their time in London. In the summer months, they retired to their country estates or visited spa towns such as Bath. The journey between London and

Bath was long and entailed overnight stops at coaching inns along the way. One of these inns was the Angel at Speenhamland, then a village but now a suburb of Newbury, Berkshire:

To Miss *Kitty F____r*, on seeing a pretty Chamber-maid of the name of *Day*, at the Sign of the *Angel* at *Spinham Land*, on *Wednesday*, the 10th of *September*, 1760.
The Lesser Light,
To rule the Night,
Heaven gave to Man's revolving Years;
Kit, hide thy Face
('Tis no Disgrace)
Thou art but *Night* when *Day* appears.[10]

Though her name continued to be referenced, Kitty herself had been absent from the gossip columns for the best part of a year. Other women had entered the spotlight. Why choose Kitty and not one of her contemporaries to compare Miss Day the chambermaid to, unless she was there and the writer saw Kitty and pretty, rosy-cheeked Miss Day side by side? It appears that the waggish, cruel poet wanted Kitty to know that she had been spotted at the inn, by giving such an exact date. Kitty's use of cosmetics was to blame for any imperfections on her face. It was a problem faced by many other women of Kitty's circle, not least Lady Coventry.

It had been a badly kept secret that Maria, Countess of Coventry was ill, and had been for a while. Like Kitty, the countess had faded into the background. Since her quarrel with Kitty in Hyde Park, Maria had not often been seen in public. She had made a rare appearance to watch the trial of Laurence Shirley, 4th Earl Ferrers, who was accused – and found guilty – of murdering his steward. Horace Walpole was there too and remarked on how well Maria looked for someone who was rumoured to have only weeks left to live. The Gunning sisters had both been noted beauties and Maria, in particular, a slavish follower of fashion. Testament to this was her habitual use of a skin-whitening cosmetic known as ceruse with which she painted her face. To be pale-skinned (with rouged cheeks) was the height of fashion. It showed that a woman had the means to stay indoors all day rather than be outside, working in the fields with her skin getting tanned by the sun. Every woman who used this make-up gambled with the consequences, however. The paste contained white lead. It poisoned the user and left lesions and blemishes on their skin. In a vicious circle, they then had to apply a heavier layer of ceruse to cover these. It was a destructive cosmetic and it hastened the end of Maria, Countess of Coventry's life. Her husband had tried to dissuade her from using it. Reputedly, on their honeymoon in Paris, she had followed the French fashion and whitened her face and rouged her cheeks. When Maria came down for dinner and the earl saw her, he chased her around the table, caught her and rubbed off the make-up with his handkerchief.[11]

The Countess of Coventry's immune system was weakened to a fatal degree by the toxic lead seeping through her pores. When Maria fell victim to tuberculosis, the disease took hold quickly and she deteriorated with a suddenness that took her family by surprise. In the autumn of 1760, at Croome Court (the Coventry's stately home in Worcestershire), Maria died. Her death was a shock. Horace Walpole said that:

Poor Lady Coventry concluded her short race with the same attention to her looks. She lay constantly on a couch with a pocket glass in her hand, and when that told her how great the change was, she took to her bed the last fortnight, had no light in her room but the lamp of a tea-kettle, and at last took things in through the curtains of her bed, without suffering them to be undrawn. The mob who never quitted curiosity about her, went, to the number of ten thousand, only to see her coffin. If she had lived to ninety like Helen, I believe they would have thought that her wrinkles deserved an epic poem. Poor thing! how far from ninety! She was not eight and twenty![12]

Lady Coventry's demise should have served as a wake-up call to the many other women of the *demimonde* who painted their faces with the same whitening make-up, Kitty among them. Jane Sumner was another who had damaged her looks. Her overuse of ceruse left her complexion 'pebbled', as one contemporary writer described it. Perhaps the shock of Maria's death had something to do with Kitty's desire to lead a more simple, private life? However, while Kitty did take a step back from her public notoriety, there was a more honest reason. For the first time since Anthony George Martin had abandoned her, Kitty had fallen in love. If she had been more shrewd, she might have continued on her path and hoped to be showered with money and gems by wealthy men. She might also have tried her best to gain a marriage proposal from someone rich enough to provide every luxury she could ever desire. It would have been the sensible option for a woman of Kitty's profession. To throw everything away for love, when there was little or no immediate return in terms of either money or position in society, was foolhardy in the extreme. They say, however, that love is blind, and it was noted at the time how easily Kitty lost her heart. A contemporary poem said of Kitty that, 'Full of desires she sighs for this, and that, / Her heart for ev'ry man goes pit-a-pat.' While Kitty might have had an eye on gaining a title, and certainly once aimed to snare a wealthy man, she settled instead for love, and love alone.[13]

Chapter Six

Mrs Brown: A Gentleman's Housekeeper

'Kitty repent, a settlement procure,
Retire, and keep the Bailiffs from the door.
Too well thour't known, too long you've play'd the whore,
Put up with wrinkles, and pray paint no more:
No more thour't thought a subject for the Town,
Reject Miss Kitty, for plain Mrs. Brown.'

(*The Meretriciad*, 1761)

The Honourable William Richard Chetwynd was around ten years Kitty's senior and the heir to a substantial fortune, a good estate, and a title. His father was John Chetwynd, 2nd Viscount Chetwynd of Bearhaven, an Irish peerage. The family's estate was Ingestre Hall in Staffordshire and the house had been in the family for centuries. Originally it had been an old medieval hall but it had been refashioned in the seventeenth century into a red-brick Jacobean mansion. In the following century, the grounds had been redesigned and laid out by Lancelot 'Capability' Brown. We don't know how William Chetwynd came to be introduced to Kitty, but he replaced the Earl of Sandwich in her life. He was besotted by her and seemed like the ideal catch. Except for one thing. William already had a wife. She was Elizabeth, the daughter of an Ipswich MP, and the couple had married by special licence at her father's London house in York Street, St James's Square in 1753. Even worse, while Chetwynd had every expectation of inheriting a fortune, at the time he met Kitty his finances were hard stretched to support both his family and a mistress.

Ingestre Hall was the home of William's father, and his son and heir had been given the use of one of the family's smaller manors. The Old Hall at Betley, a black and white half-timbered Tudor house, was William Chetwynd's home, only he lived there no longer. While the concept of the seven-year itch is of much later date, it does describe the Chetwynds' marriage, which had produced one daughter. William Chetwynd had tired of his wife and was looking elsewhere for his pleasures. Kitty was happy to accommodate him, despite his flaws. There is a possibility that Chetwynd may have been in Kitty's life since the time of her accident in the Mall. *The Juvenile Adventures of Miss Kitty Fisher* mentioned one further man, in its closing pages. The pseudonym given for him was Count de Demargo, but there was no description, no idea of how old he was nor his appearance. It was said that he had been married several years and that although his wife was beautiful, he had only married her for her family connections and could not bring himself to be intimate with her. The author suggested that the marriage had never been consummated and that Count de Demargo was impotent. However, if it was Chetwynd who was referenced, then he had at least slept in his wife's bed on occasion. It suggests that the gossips had already got to work unpicking the Chetwynds' marriage and that rumours had started to grow. Elizabeth's family was well connected, especially on her maternal line. Her grandfather was a Huguenot, John Francis Fauquier, who had been a wealthy director of the Bank of England. Elizabeth's uncle, Francis Fauquier, was the governor of Virginia and good friends with Thomas Jefferson. Fauquier County in Virginia is named for him. Elizabeth had no doubt brought a sizeable dowry with her when she became Mrs Chetwynd.[1]

Educated at Eton, and then at Corpus Christi College, Oxford, William Chetwynd was the MP for Stafford. He also served George II as an equerry in the latter years of the king's reign. Perhaps it had been William Chetwynd with whom Kitty visited Bath in the summer of 1760? They may have been together for a year at that point. The publication of *The Juvenile Adventures* did have that catastrophic effect on her life which Kitty feared. It scared away her suitors and, worse, it ultimately removed her mystique. The sleazy side of Kitty's life as a 'celebrated courtesan' had been laid bare, a layer of magic stripped away. Whether the story was true or false mattered little, as people believed it and that was what counted. Kitty had been painted as a gold-digger, with a background as a common harlot. Her carefully cultivated image fell apart and the portraits had yet to work their magic. Living in the full glare of publicity lost its charms and the Honourable Mr Chetwynd offered a new beginning. While still known as a courtesan, Kitty became more his lover than a kept woman. In any case, Chetwynd couldn't afford to keep someone like Kitty Fisher in any great style. She could expect no riches, no grand equipage. There can be only one reason that Kitty would give up everything for Chetwynd. He was the man she wanted to be with, regardless of his lack of ready cash and the fact that he had a wife and child back in Staffordshire. She had refused a similar set-up with Earl Poulett, who had wanted to hide Kitty away at Hinton House. With Chetwynd, at least there was love and romance. They lived quietly, man and wife in name if nothing else, just as Kitty had done with Anthony George Martin. Chetwynd didn't flaunt Kitty and wasn't prepared to share her with other men. Quite simply, Kitty had fallen in love, and she turned her back on both her short-lived celebrity and her career as a courtesan.

Chetwynd took the lease on a country estate as a home for Kitty and himself. This wasn't quite as grand as it sounds. Titsey Place was a tumbledown, ancient manor house near Oxted in Surrey. The owner, Sir John Gresham, let it out rather than live there and the house was the best that Chetwynd could afford while staying within easy reach of the capital. While the house might not have been in tip-top condition, the grounds and surrounding countryside more than made up for the fact. The old manor was sheltered beneath the tree-lined grassy slopes of Botley Hill, the highest point on the North Downs. The location was beautiful and the air was pure, sweet, and delicate.

At the heart of Kitty's manor house stood an old, once-grand hall with stained glass windows featuring the Gresham family's arms and crest complete with their emblem, a golden grasshopper on a green mound. Dark, dusty oak panelling carved with fruit, flowers, and 'strange Moorish' heads lined the walls and above, a gallery ran around, part of which made a galleried chamber. The arched wooden beams, and creaking floorboards, were the antithesis of the Palladian and Neo-Classical styles that were in vogue at the time. On either side of this central building was a two-storey wing. One had two parlours, a kitchen, brewhouse, washhouse, laundry, and dairy on the ground floor and upstairs were the bedrooms, a dressing room and various closets. The other wing consisted of stabling plus a hayloft and granaries. The grounds were laid out with fishponds, a well-planted orchard, a dovecot, and a pleasant garden. Eight acres of meadows surrounded the secluded house, which Chetwynd and Kitty took unfurnished. The lease had been advertised in the summer of 1759, and they possibly moved in not many months afterwards. This, then, was the reason for Kitty's sudden disappearance from the gossip columns. She had been spirited away and was happily playing the role of a country squire's wife in complete privacy, apart from the few servants retained to help run the estate.[2]

Despite living at Titsey Place, Kitty kept her London townhouse. It was a base for visits to the capital and her family. Chetwynd, as an MP and king's equerry, would need to pay occasional visits to parliament and the royal court. Taxation records for Norfolk Street show that Kitty continued to use Anthony George Martin's surname as her own. However, she spent little time there. Joshua Reynolds's pocketbooks record only three sittings for Kitty during 1760, one on 2 February and then the other two on Christmas Day and New Year's Eve. Chetwynd, it appears, must have returned to Staffordshire, to spend the holiday season with his wife and daughter. Kitty, then, probably viewed a return to London as preferable to rattling around in the large manor house on her own. As she was at a loose end, the notoriously hard-working Reynolds took advantage of Kitty's reappearance in the capital. A few weeks earlier, the artist had also moved to a new home, 47 Leicester Fields. In time, he would build an extension at the rear for a studio and gallery but that Christmas, his studio was squeezed into one of the rooms on the four floors of his house. It was a step up and, although only a stone's throw away from Reynolds's previous address, a much better one.

By the following summer, London was all busy excitement. Shortly after Maria, Countess of Coventry's demise, George II had also died and his eldest – and namesake – grandson had taken the crown. Maria never got to see a coronation, but Kitty was about to get the chance. The new king had also just announced the news of his wedding. George III was a young man, just 22, and his chosen bride was a German princess, Charlotte of Mecklenburg-Strelitz. Both wedding and the coronation ceremony were scheduled to take place in the autumn, within two weeks of each other. London was in a frenzy, and all available rooms were booked up. Crowds descended upon the capital to catch a glimpse of their new queen, and to watch the coronation procession to Westminster Abbey. There were firework displays planned, dances, and lavish feasts. Surely Kitty wanted to witness something of the occasion and make one of the many who lined the route?

In the meantime, rumours appeared in the newspapers concerning a society wedding. The widowed Earl of Coventry was reported to have married again, to the beautiful Barbara St John, daughter of the 11th Baron St John of Bletso. The news was premature. Lord Coventry and Barbara did marry, but not for another three years. Instead, the woman on Lord Coventry's arm in the summer of 1761 was Mary 'Polly' Davis, reputedly born in a wheelbarrow in Covent Garden. Polly aimed to be Kitty's successor in the celebrity stakes but she was a pale imitation of the celebrated Kitty Fisher. Polly had no refinement or good manners, for one thing.[3]

On a warm evening in late July, Lord Coventry and Polly strolled arm-in-arm around Ranelagh Gardens. Polly was a year or two younger than Kitty and enjoying the attention. The earl was not the first of Polly's conquests; she had been William Chetwynd's lover before he turned his eyes towards Kitty. When Polly saw Kitty and Chetwynd walking past, she worked herself up into an angry, jealous rage. There were a few choice words thrown about and then Polly came out fighting. A scuffle ensued, to the amusement of those nearby. Polly launched herself at Kitty and landed a blow on her head. Lord Coventry intervened, earning himself a slap across the face from an irate Polly. Guards ran across and before she could do any more harm, Polly was thrown out of the gardens and told she was barred. Kitty was mortified to find herself the injured party in a common catfight. Elizabeth, Countess (later Duchess) of Northumberland was one of the interested bystanders who had witnessed the debacle. She went home and recorded the events of the evening in her diary, disparaging Kitty as just a 'very pretty woman of the town' who was kept by Chetwynd. A satirical pamphlet that mentioned Kitty was published soon after. It was called *The Meretriciad* and was a satire written in verse by Captain Edward Thompson of the navy. In this publication, Kitty's charms were praised alongside those of her fellow courtesans (Jane Sumner was also mentioned within its pages). 'Poet Thompson', as he became known, moved in literary as well as naval circles. He was well-placed to hear first-hand the gossip about Kitty and her contemporaries. *The Meretriciad*, Thompson's first work, was written while he was between commands and on the half-pay. It was a huge success and went through around six editions. The contretemps at Ranelagh was recounted:[4]

> O pretty *Poll!* will nought thy ire restrain;
> Must a poor Muse for *Kitty* plead in vain?
> Won't all the powers of *Renelagh* withstand
> The little ruin of thy little hand?
> O shame, Miss *Polly*, to thy worshipp'd face!
> Not to regard the grandeur of the place;
> But rush to battle without fear of care,
> Nor spare my Lord – nor spare his Lady's hair;

O what a body! with a soul so big!
To beat the powder from a Noble's wig;
Great was the conquest in that awful place,
But oh! the exit, was a dire disgrace.

Kitty tried her best to ignore pamphlets such as *The Meretriciad*. She no longer relished her celebrity and preferred to remain out of the public's notice. The fact that William Chetwynd was unable to offer marriage didn't bother Kitty. She was happy to live with him in the seclusion of the Surrey countryside. In practical terms, it was a more economical way of life, as well as affording privacy. The couple opted for a simpler lifestyle that suited Kitty. She always loved the outdoors and now there were walks and rides on her doorstep. The tranquillity was soothing. Besides, Kitty was in love and, as Chetwynd seems to have been faithful to her, perhaps he was too. Given the personal commitment between them, perhaps Kitty hoped that one day William might be free to marry and make her Catherine, Viscountess Chetwynd? For that to happen, however, the current Mrs Chetwynd would have to depart her life. While divorce was possible, it was not an easy process. William needed his wife to take the initiative and sue for a divorce due to her husband's infidelity. However, this would take away all her security and rights as Chetwynd's wife. The best course of revenge for Elizabeth was to do nothing. Unless she was emulating her husband and entertaining a lover – and could be caught in the act – it would be nigh on impossible for Chetwynd to free himself from his marriage.

Unfortunately for Kitty, there is no evidence that the abandoned Mrs Chetwynd was anything less than an exemplary wife. However, Chetwynd's affair with Kitty gave his wider family cause for concern. He was the heir and needed a son to inherit after him. John Chetwynd, 2nd Viscount Chetwynd was William's father, and four children had been born to him, two boys and two girls. The eldest son had died young and so all his father's ambitions rested on William's shoulders.

If Kitty's lover had no son to follow him then the title and estate would be separated. Did she dream of giving Chetwynd that wished-for son?

In an attempt to quell gossip, Kitty passed as William Chetwynd's housekeeper and assumed yet another name. She called herself Mrs Brown. It was not an uncommon ruse, and Chetwynd was not alone in referring to his mistress as his housekeeper in an attempt to give a veneer of respectability. At the same time, another woman had adopted an identical pseudonym. Mary Banks, a relation of the great naturalist Sir Joseph Banks, was known to one and all as Mrs Brown, the 5th Duke of Bolton's housekeeper. In reality, Mary Banks Brown (she adopted the surname as an additional one) was the duke's mistress and mother of his child. What went on behind the closed doors of country estates and London townhouses largely stayed behind them. The servants knew better than to pass comment in public on their masters and mistresses, at least if they wished to keep their jobs.[5]

The newspapers which had tittle-tattled on the scandals of Kitty's life fell silent about her life at Titsey Place. The only source that tells of Kitty at this time is *The Meretriciad* and it was this work that immortalised Kitty as Mrs Brown. 'Poet Thompson' didn't think much of Kitty's lover, for he gave William Chetwynd a withering character appraisal:

> Thy man's a bankrupt both in purse and lust;
> And tho' the Sun shines, yet may fortune frown,
> And quite reduce, both him, and Mrs Brown.
> Mankind's deceitful, you have had your swing,
> Remember L__k_t wore a brilliant ring.
> Kitty repent, a settlement procure,
> Retire, and keep the Bailiffs from the door,
> Too well thou'rt known, too long you've play'd the whore,
> Put up with wrinkles, and pray paint no more:
> No more thou'rt thought a subject for the Town,
> Reject Miss Kitty, for plain Mrs Brown.[6]

With hindsight, Kitty would have been wise to take Thompson's advice but not for the reasons offered. Besides, it's unlikely that Chetwynd would have been able to make any kind of financial settlement. He was heir to a viscountcy but was no rich peer with a fortune to squander. However, Kitty was happy to enjoy a few years of peaceful semi-respectability and quasi-connubial bliss. It was an echo of her earlier happiness as Mrs Martin before being abandoned by her Military Cupid. Titsey Place was Kitty's haven and she was content. The years spent there were, perhaps, the happiest of her life.

In *The Meretriciad*, Thompson connects Kitty Fisher with Lucy Lockit. Lucy was a character in John Gay's play, *The Beggar's Opera*, which premiered in 1728. Thompson said, 'Remember L__k_t wore a brilliant ring'. Lucy Lockit believed herself betrothed to the notorious and womanising highwayman, Macheath, but Macheath was already married. His secret wife was Polly Peachum, daughter of the unscrupulous leader of a gang of thieves and prostitutes. (Mr Peachum turned his gang over to the authorities as and when they stopped earning him enough money.) Thompson's readers would understand the reference. Lucy's rival, Polly Peachum, despite being married to Macheath, was kept secret and called his housekeeper while Lucy Lockit, the woman who had the prior claim on the highwayman, was left unwed. In a back-to-front parallel to the play, with the roles reversed, it was Mrs Elizabeth Chetwynd (aka Lucy Lockit) who had been abandoned. Kitty (who Thompson compared to Polly Peachum) was living with Chetwynd as his wife in all but name and known as Titsey Place's housekeeper, Mrs Brown. In *The Beggar's Opera*, Mrs Peachum asked her daughter if she would support Macheath by 'Gaming, Drinking, and Whoring'. Was Thompson trying to suggest that Kitty, far from being kept by her lover, was having to support Chetwynd financially, using up any money she had saved from her time as a courtesan? As for the man himself, highwayman antics aside, it seems that Thompson thought Chetwynd was otherwise comparable to the scurrilous rake, Macheath. Kitty didn't care. She was in love and blind to Chetwynd's flaws.

Selected quotes from *The Beggar's Opera*:

ACT 4, Scene 1

LUCY LOCKIT: But Love, Sir, is a Misfortune that may happen to the most discreet Woman, and in Love we are all Fools alike. Notwithstanding all that he swore, I am now fully convinc'd that Polly Peachum is actually his Wife. Did I let him escape (Fool that I was!) to go to her? Polly will wheedle herself into his Money…

ACT 4, Scene 7

LUCY LOCKIT: Jealousy, Rage, Love and Fear are at once tearing me to pieces, How am I weather-beaten and shatter'd with Distresses!

I'm like a Skiff on the Ocean tost,

Now high, now low, with each Billow born,

With her Rudder broke, and her Anchor lost,

Deserted and all forlorn.

While thus I lie rolling and tossing all Night,

That Polly lies sporting on seas of Delight!

ACT 4, Scene 8

LUCY LOCKIT: … Ah Polly! Polly! 'tis I am the unhappy Wife; and he loves you as if you were only his Mistress.

POLLY PEACHUM: Sure, Madam, you cannot think me so happy as to be the object of your Jealousy. A Man is always afraid of a Woman who loves him too well, so that I must expect to be neglected and avoided.

LUCY LOCKIT: Then our Cases, my dear Polly, are exactly alike. Both of us indeed have been too fond.

The invisibility of Chetwynd and Kitty during their time together suggests that with the Seven Years' War at an end and diplomatic relations with France restored, they perhaps left the country for a time. In mainland Europe, their money would stretch further and Kitty's reputation would not be such a bar to being received in polite society. France, in particular, viewed a woman such as Kitty in a very different light. The French court had, over the years, been partially governed by a succession of the monarch's paramours. These women had even been given a semi-official position within the royal palaces of France. They were known by the title of *maîtresse-en-titre*, the chief royal mistress. In Samuel Foote's play, *A Trip to Calais*, written almost twenty years later, one of the characters travels with his wife but introduces her as his mistress to appear fashionable. Chetwynd and Kitty would be accepted as a couple more readily on mainland Europe where public perception was more relaxed. If Kitty did travel abroad, then her life was similar in that respect to one of her contemporaries. The voluptuous and beautiful Nancy Parsons had taken over where Kitty left off in terms of being London's most desirable courtesan.

Anne (better known as Nancy) Parsons was born in the 1730s and said to be the daughter of a Bond Street tailor. A later account claimed that Nancy was of a good family but small fortune, and she had always moved in polite society. Horace Walpole, on the other hand, described Nancy as a prostitute who had also acted in minor roles on stage at the opera. Like Kitty, Nancy altered the whole course of her life when she fell in love. Nancy's choice was a Mr Haughton, a West Indian slave merchant. When Haughton invited Nancy to accompany him to the Caribbean, she jumped at the chance. In Jamaica, at Haughton's estate (where a grand house was being built), Nancy was introduced as Mrs Haughton. It was a ruse which fooled few people for, just as Kitty had called herself Mrs Martin, it was an assumed title and there had been no marriage. Haughton either died or Nancy tired of him, depending on which version of her story you believe. Whatever the truth, Nancy returned to England with little more to show for her overseas adventures than a new surname. She took lodgings above Cooper's perfumery shop in Soho, on the corner of Brewer Street and Golden Square. Thereafter, Nancy was known as Mrs Horton (or Houghton), but London society gossip soon discredited her pretended marital status.[7]

While Kitty was hidden in the Surrey countryside, Nancy began her career as a courtesan. By 1764, she was the talk of the town when she snared Augustus Fitzroy, 3rd Duke of Grafton, as her lover. He was the peer rumoured to have been Maria, Countess of Coventry's lover. Though he was married, Grafton flaunted Nancy as his mistress. Even worse, Grafton's wife (the same woman who had complained about Kitty sitting near her at the theatre) was pregnant at the time. Scandal followed scandal while Nancy presided at the duke's side at social functions. He became First Minister in 1767 and Nancy acted as his consort at parties and social gatherings. In something of a paradox, given her distaste for Kitty, the discarded Duchess of Grafton went on to take a lover herself (John FitzPatrick, 2nd Earl of Ossory), by whom she had a child. The duke divorced his errant wife, heedless of the irony of the situation, and Nancy expected him to offer her a duchess's coronet. She was disappointed. Three months after his divorce, the Duke of Grafton married Elizabeth Wrottesley, the Dean of Worcester's daughter. Status and the prospect of a dowry trumped the sexual favours and charms of a courtesan nearly every time.[8]

Nancy's obvious ability to host a dinner party and to entertain the duke's aristocratic friends gives the lie to Walpole's description of her as a common prostitute and opera girl. Nancy, like Kitty, had received a good education and been brought up with a knowledge of etiquette. Both women had the manners and wit to hold their own in polite society. However, there was one big difference between the two women. Nancy may have been cultured but she was always a courtesan at heart. The reason the duke had spurned her after his divorce was because he had discovered that Nancy had been conducting an affair behind his back. Nancy's secret lover was the handsome – and much younger – John Frederick Sackville, 3rd Duke of Dorset. Horace Walpole witheringly referred to Nancy as 'the Duke of Grafton's Mrs Houghton, the Duke of Dorset's Mrs Houghton, everybody's Mrs Houghton!'

At last, in 1776, Nancy snared a marriage proposal from her latest beau, Charles Maynard, 2nd Viscount Maynard. She still didn't settle down into middle-aged respectability, though. She was a courtesan to the end. In Italy, in the mid-1780s and when Nancy was in her 50s, the Maynards began a curious *ménage à trois* with the 19-year-old Francis Russell, 5th Duke of Bedford. By the end of her life, Nancy, Viscountess Maynard was drifting – solo – around mainland Europe. She died outside Paris either in late 1814 or early 1815.

While Nancy's fame in London was at its height, Kitty was content to pass as nobody more consequential than Chetwynd's faux housekeeper. Kitty was most definitely not born to be a courtesan, despite being remembered as one of history's most famous. When she settled down with a man, Kitty was constant to him. A loving monogamous relationship was now the pinnacle of her ambition. Let the likes of Nancy Parsons steal her thunder, Kitty cared not. A little bit older and wiser, she craved anonymity. Kitty had always used an alias to hide her true identity. She was Mrs Brown, Mrs Martin, or Kitty Fisher. Behind closed doors, however, Chetwynd grew to know the real woman, Catherine Maria Fischer.

Her infamous past never disappeared, though, as much as she tried to put it behind her. Kitty found herself, reluctantly, propelled into public notoriety once again. The earliest edition of *Harris's List* to have survived is the one for 1761. We do not know if Kitty was mentioned in the former ones. She was, however, named in that 1761 copy of *Harris's List*, but in a different way to the other women and girls advertised within its pages. The editors alleged that Kitty had sent them a letter, pleading with them not to list her. 'Though brought to misfortunes,' Kitty's letter said, she 'never yet was on the common'. Included with the letter, it was claimed, was a bribe of five guineas. Had Kitty been told that she was going to be listed in the directory, and attempted to negotiate her way out of its pages? Or was her still-famous name merely used as a ruse to increase publicity? It was a scheme that others made use of. The following year, another pamphlet bearing Kitty's name hit the streets, priced at one shilling. It claimed to be *A Sketch of the Present Times, and the Times to Come in an Address to Kitty Fisher* and, in verse, foretold a dismal future for Kitty when her looks and sex appeal had diminished. Unless, that is, Kitty repented. The anonymous author was, at least, honest about its intent and why Kitty's name was used:[9]

> But mind not, dear KITTY, that ignoble Crew
> Who pretend to make Writing their Trade;
> Why, they'll rail at their Maker, as soon as at you,
> Provided they cou'd but be paid.
> Grub-street eccho'd from Garrets, we'll write and we'll eat,
> They knew, that Desire with you chose to dwell;
> So inventive Necessity taught them the cheat,
> That your Name to a Pamphlet wou'd make the Trash sell.[10]

Though her name was appropriated in this way, Kitty herself remained absent from the gossip columns. Her occasional visits to London were made under society's gossipy radar and the prime reason for them, besides seeing her family, was to sit for another portrait. Kitty remained a regular visitor to Joshua Reynolds's house and studio in Leicester Fields. These sittings were for a portrait in which she is painted seated, one dove on her lap and another by her shoulder, perched on the back of her chair. Engravings of this painting appeared later in the year. Perhaps Reynolds and Kitty did have an agreement that they would share the profits arising from the sales of prints? A little extra cash would be welcome, to prop up Kitty and Chetwynd's life at Titsey Place. Three original versions of this portrait are known to be in existence, each subtly different from one another. The Kitty depicted in all three is, however, a different woman from the knowing courtesan of her first portraits. She looks wistful, lost in thought. Reynolds painted Kitty almost in profile, her gaze directed to a point off the canvas. This is in direct contrast to the first of his paintings of Kitty where she is looking, challengingly, into the eyes of the viewer. Her pink dress, edged with fur, symbolises her femininity and hints at romance. Around Kitty's neck in two of the paintings is a locket containing a miniature portrait of a man. He is different in each; one may depict William Chetwynd. In the third portrait – which is thought to have been completed at a much later date – the fur on Kitty's dress is ermine and the locket is missing.[11]

Reynolds executed several other paintings of Kitty during her lifetime, or at least ones reputed to be of her. The dates for these are obscure and there are no details as to who commissioned them. Belvoir Castle in Rutland had one which, decades later, hung on the wall of the dressing room used by the Prince Regent when he visited. It was lost along with several others, consumed in a devastating blaze at the castle on an October night in 1816. Another portrait shows Kitty sitting in a chair, wearing a silvery blue dress and holding a fan. This portrait ended up in South Africa. There is one more unfinished portrait of Kitty Fisher by Reynolds which dates from this period of her life. In it, Kitty appears more natural with an air of innocence, but still sensual. Her glossy chestnut brown hair is unpowdered and she lounges in an armchair in a state of *déshabillé*, transfixed by a parrot perched on one of her outstretched hands. It is thought to be Reynolds's pet bird. This Kitty looks younger, more her true age (she would be around 21 or 22 years old). The viewer is given the impression they have almost caught Kitty unawares, that they are spying on a private and intimate moment. The woman in this portrait is more Catherine Maria Fischer than Kitty Fisher. She is the woman whom William Chetwynd knew as his own. To view it together with Reynolds's earlier paintings of Kitty is to see her dilemma. Across the paintings, Kitty is presented at all points between the modest woman hoping for her happy-ever-after and the artful courtesan who sold her body to the highest bidder to pay her bills. Like the Cleopatra portrait, this one also appears to have remained in Reynolds's studio during Kitty's lifetime.[12]

A constant stream of the great, the fashionable, and the notorious came and went from Joshua Reynolds's door. One other woman who also sat to the painter at this time became known as a rival to Kitty Fisher. She was Nelly O'Brien, another 'celebrated courtesan'. Nelly was Kitty's neighbour when she was in London and lived just a few doors further down Norfolk Street, in one of the smaller houses on the less fashionable eastern side. Both Kitty and Nelly sat to Reynolds in the first half of the 1760s. (Nelly, like Kitty before her, was said to have been introduced to Reynolds by Admiral Augustus Keppel, 1st Viscount Keppel.) Did Kitty Fisher and Nelly O'Brien ever bump into each other on their journeys between Norfolk Street and Reynolds's studio? Or acknowledge one another through the windows of their carriages, as they travelled along the dusty London streets? Reynolds's two portraits of Nelly were both paid for by her lover, Frederick St John, 2nd Viscount Bolingbroke. While Reynolds's brush was busy capturing Kitty and Nelly's beauty, he was also painting Bolingbroke's wife, Diana, Lady Bolingbroke, née Spencer (the Duke of Marlborough's eldest daughter). It is rumoured that Bolingbroke asked Reynolds to give his wife's eyes 'something of Nelly O'Brien'. Horace Walpole wickedly related the anecdote, adding that as Bolingbroke had 'given Nelly something of his wife's, it was but fair to give her something of Nelly's; and my Lady will not throw away the present!' In both her portraits, Nelly stares out directly. One shows her seated, holding a small white lapdog. She is dressed in a blue and white striped gown, open at the front to reveal a pink quilted petticoat, overlaid with a gauzy apron. A black lace shawl sits around her shoulders, and a pearl necklace and straw bonnet complete her outfit. In the second painting, Nelly adopts a classical pose, seated in a loose pink gown and leaning back against a pillar.

The portraits might both have been paid for by Bolingbroke, but while they were being painted, Nelly had moved on. Her new lover was Sackville Tufton, 8th Earl of Thanet. By the end of 1764, Nelly had given Tufton a son, Alfred, and had left Norfolk Street to reign supreme at her lover's townhouse in Grosvenor Square. Much good it did her, though. By the summer of 1767, when she was pregnant for the third time (a second son, Sackville, had been born late in 1765), Nelly was turned away from Grosvenor Square. Instead, she was given a more modest lodging on Park Street. With Nelly out of the way, Tufton married an heiress, Mary, daughter of Lord John Sackville. Nelly was furious at having to leave Grosvenor Square. She complained to anyone who would listen that her former lover should have behaved as the Duke of Grafton had done. When the wife of Augustus Fitzroy, 3rd Duke of Grafton was pregnant, the duke had moved Nancy Parsons into his London home. The Earl of Thanet had instead moved his courtesan out. In the end, though, both Nelly and Nancy found themselves cast adrift.[13]

It's interesting to compare Kitty Fisher's career with that of Nelly O'Brien and Nancy Parsons. The latter two kept on trading up their keepers, rather than staying constant to one man. They looked for money and all the luxuries it would bring into their lives. In the case of Nelly, she hoped to gain future security by bearing children to her lovers. Meanwhile, Kitty sacrificed all for love and there were never rumours of any pregnancies in her life. Kitty now packed up her belongings and left Norfolk Street. She was no longer the 'celebrated courtesan' of a year or so earlier and the expensive house overlooking Hyde Park had become an unaffordable luxury. William Chetwynd was in no position to pay for anything as grand. Instead, Kitty took over her father's lease on a smaller house in nearby Mayfair for which Kitty had probably been paying the rent, anyway. It was on the not-quite-as-fashionable Carrington Street, a narrow thoroughfare in a maze of roads and mews containing carriage houses and stabling close to Piccadilly. The street formed part of the site of the Shepherd

Market, a newly gentrified area where the old and infamous fifteen-day May Fair had been held for centuries. Insignificant and easy to overlook, Carrington Street was still close enough to Piccadilly that it could be considered a good address. John Henry Fischer's name had been on the lease for the previous twelve months. Now, however, his health was failing and the Fischer family turned to Kitty for protection. Carrington Street was her parents and younger siblings' home, and Kitty now stayed there too when she visited London. Neither too downmarket nor too grand, it was perfect. The once infamous Kitty could slip in and out almost unnoticed, but she probably spent less and less time in the capital. Sir Joshua Reynolds's pocketbook for 1763 is missing, so we don't know if she sat for him during that year. Kitty, did, however, have her portrait painted in miniature, by the Irish-born artist, Luke Sullivan.[14]

Sullivan had once been an engraver and worked as Hogarth's assistant. Although more than thirty years Kitty's senior, he was known as a ladies' man. The sculptor, Joseph Nollekens, Sullivan's contemporary, thought him a 'handsome, lively fellow'. Sullivan flattered his sitters, flirted with them and captured beautiful and often intimate portraits as a result. His miniature of Kitty is no exception. Surely it was William Chetwynd who commissioned this portrait? Kitty is painted wearing a green dress, with a pink wrap draped around her shoulders and matching ribbons in her hair. She wears no jewellery and her appearance is simple. Kitty is painted as a contented lover and not an accomplished courtesan. In the background are trees, and Kitty is leaning against the trunk of one. Perhaps the setting represents the grounds of Titsey Place? In her arms, Kitty cradles a small black and white lapdog.[15]

Kitty seems to have spent an inordinate amount of time in artists' studios. Besides the multitude of Reynolds's portraits and Sullivan's miniature, other portraits exist – or have been known to exist – that claim to depict her. Portraits by William Hogarth have been rumoured, and another by Thomas Gainsborough where Kitty – if it is she – is almost in profile, dressed in a brown muslin dress, a white chemisette over her shoulders and a mob cap upon her head. Less than a decade after Kitty's death, a miniature by the renowned Richard Cosway was sold, depicting her in the character of a Magdalen (repentant prostitute). In the late eighteenth century, a miniature of Kitty by Rupert Barber passed through a London auction house and, in the twentieth century, another by Ozias Humphry was exhibited. Only a select few of the portraits of Kitty went on to be engraved. Some must have been intended for private ownership rather than public consumption.[16]

Back in Surrey, unwanted public attention was about to catch up with Kitty once more. This time, it was a scandal in which she was an innocent party, however. Kitty had dismissed one of her coachmen. Nothing remains to say whether she had concerns about the man's character or whether she was just saving money by letting him go. However, events might lead one to suspect it was the former, and that Kitty was well rid of her servant. He was Matthew Dodd, a married man with a young family. Leaving Titsey Place, Dodd set off on the road uphill towards Croydon, intending to get a job as a country carrier. Before he found a new employer though, Dodd hit the headlines. He was accused of committing a terrible crime. Poor Kitty's name was dragged into the story by the gutter press. They knew that calling Dodd 'Kitty's Fisher's coachman' would generate interest to sell their broadsheets. The *Public Advertiser* was a bit more discreet in reporting the story, as far as Kitty was concerned, at least. It said that 'A Few days ago, the late Coachman of a celebrated Courtezan pulled a young woman from her horse, on Warlingham Lane near Croydon, and ravished her, for which offence he has since been apprehended, and committed to Gaol.'[17]

The young woman was Anne Dutnall, a 19-year-old farmer's daughter. She had been riding along a lane that led from the village of Warlingham towards Croydon when Dodd chanced upon her. He dragged Anne towards some woodland while she screamed, 'Murder!'

but there was no one around to hear. It was only a few miles away from Titsey Place. Had Dodd left in a temper and taken out his rage on Anne instead of Kitty? His attack on Anne was brutal (it was reported that Dodd throttled the girl to subdue her, before raping her). Over six weeks later, Anne was still suffering from her injuries, both physical and mental. It was reported that she 'lies very ill, at her Father's House near Croydon'. Dodd protested he was innocent of the crime but, at his trial, he was found guilty and sentenced to hang on Kennington Common. The addition of Kitty's name into the sordid saga, even though she was blameless, piqued the public's interest.

Dodd's execution was delayed for a week while his friends and family tried to obtain a pardon for him. He maintained that he did not deserve to die. When the day of his execution dawned, a tremendous storm blew in. A gale howled around the walls of the New Gaol on Horsemonger Lane in Southwark and rain lashed down, soaking the mob gathered outside. Dodd, together with the other condemned prisoners, was taken from his cell and placed in carts. The angry crowd at the prison's gate refused to let the carts leave. They were worked into a frenzy by the sound of Dodd's wife from an adjoining house, her tormented shrieks and wails echoing in the wind. Facing what looked like a growing rebellion and rescue attempt, the authorities called for reinforcements. A detachment of 150 soldiers with fixed bayonets marched from the Tower of London to the New Gaol and kept the crowds at bay as the journey to the gallows was restarted. In living memory, never had a hanging taken place so late in the day on the Common; it was almost 7.00 pm before Dodd had the noose around his neck. Kitty Fisher's coachman was no more. There was one more twist to Dodd's story, though. The whole sorry tale reached the ears of the king, who was alarmed by the insurrection. Two days after Dodd's execution, George III sent for the prime minister, George Grenville. Among the issues the king wanted to discuss was how to 'restrain the licentiousness of the times'. He was horrified that people had tried to prevent the execution of a criminal.

It was, said the king, 'time a remedy should be found to these evils, for that if he suffered force to be put upon him by the Opposition, the mob would try to govern him next.' The route from Titsey Place to Carrington Street took Kitty past Kennington Common. Every time she travelled to the capital after Dodd's crime, she was reminded of his terrible deeds. She was guiltless but even so, if Dodd had been sacked, Kitty must have felt the horror of having innocently set in motion the chain of events.[18]

A few months later, rumours once again spread concerning Kitty. Gossips on the London streets whispered that 'the celebrated Miss Kitty Fisher' had married 'a very eminent dealer in horses and master of a great livery-stable near May-Fair'. No doubt Kitty had been spotted in Mayfair's Carrington Street, but she had not married the keeper of a stable nor anyone else. She was still Mrs Brown, Chetwynd's nominal housekeeper. Unlike most housekeepers, however, she continued to sit for portraits, acting as a muse to Joshua Reynolds. The following year, on a warm July day, Kitty once again visited his home. Reynolds had been out of London for some weeks, at Blenheim Palace painting the portraits of the young Duke and Duchess of Marlborough. Kitty was the first visitor to Reynolds's studio on his return. The friendship between Reynolds and Kitty was strong and long-lasting.[19]

Any money worries that Kitty and Chetwyn had were alleviated a little when Chetwynd was appointed Master of the Tennis Court by George III in May 1764. In that position, he was responsible for the upkeep of the royal tennis courts at Hampton Court. In return, Chetwynd had the use of any profits arising from both the courts and the apartments belonging to them. It gave the couple just enough to live upon and Kitty took the lease on another London base, on Bruton Street, which opened onto Berkeley Square. As a measure of some independence and security, it was a wise move to have the property in her name. Bruton Street was a place to see and be seen, not least at the nearby confectionery shop run by Domenico Negri under the sign of 'The Pot and Pineapple'. Negri was an Italian pastry cook but he made more than sweetmeats. The main attraction at the Pot and Pineapple were flavoured ices. The shop overlooked Berkeley Square's central 3½ acre enclosed oblong garden, set with shady trees. If Kitty wanted, she could park outside Domenico Negri's shop in her carriage and a waiter would run out with her order. Perhaps, with Chetwynd's royal appointment and his favour with George III, the couple were intending to try to establish themselves within society, despite Kitty's position as a mistress?[20]

However, all too soon Kitty must have guessed that her contented lifestyle was coming to an end. It became obvious that William Chetwynd was unwell. He grew thin and weak, racked with an ever-present cough. Chetwynd was wasting away before Kitty's eyes and the cause was the same disease which had carried off Maria, Countess of Coventry. William Chetwynd was dying of consumption. As his breaths shortened and he started to cough up blood, Kitty's role became more that of a nurse than a lover. During the winter of 1764, Chetwynd travelled to the south of France in a last-ditch attempt to prolong his life. Although no travelling companions are mentioned, surely Kitty would have been at his side, nursing her lover through what she knew was a fatal illness? She was no doubt reminded of the death of John Henderson's brother in Paddington when she was just a girl. Chetwynd and Kitty prayed that a warmer, drier climate would work a miracle and give Chetwynd a little more time. He made it to the south coast of France but there the Honourable William Richard Chetwynd died. He was 33 years old. His death was reported in the English newspapers in late February.[21]

If Kitty was in southern France with Chetwynd, she was soon faced with an almost insurmountable problem. The plan was for Chetwynd's body to be returned to England for burial, and so it was embalmed and placed in a sturdy lead-lined coffin, ready for the journey. The couple had been living on credit, however. Six weeks after his death, Chetwynd's coffin had only made it as far as Paris before his debts overtook the little funeral procession. The Parisian authorities detained Chetwynd's corpse, placing it in the Protestant burial ground near the Hôpital Saint-Louis. There he quite possibly remains to this day.[22]

Back in England, Kitty was once again forced to fend for herself. Kitty had known Chetwynd was dying. She also knew that, after his death, she would be left with very little. Chetwynd had nothing to bequeath her of any great worth. He left no will, and anything he did own became his wife Elizabeth's property. Kitty needed to spirit away the possessions she thought she was entitled to after spending over five years by Chetwynd's side, reigning as the mistress of Titsey Place. For a time, she returned to the old manor house, full of memories of happier days. There she could temporarily hide from real life and mourn the man she had loved.

Back in London, her parents and sisters still lived at Carrington Street, but in that house too there was sadness. Sickness was stalking Kitty, and her father's illness had taken a turn for the worse. Kitty had no option but to try to support her family, both emotionally and financially. Her two sisters, Anne and Sarah Louisa, were 20 and 18 respectively. Their school days were over and they were left in an odd position. These younger Fischer girls lived in the fashionable end of town but did so at the charity of their sister. At the same time, Kitty's reputation tarnished their own. As soon as Anne and Sarah stepped through their front door, they felt the disapproving glances of their neighbours. With Kitty's example before them, they may have considered following in her footsteps, but they did have other options. The younger Fischer girls had a good boarding school education, and so they could have tried for a position as a governess, or schoolmistress, and hoped Kitty's name could be kept quiet. Perhaps, as Kitty once had, they considered work in a milliner's shop or as a dressmaker? If, however, they viewed a career in the upper echelons of London's sex trade with temptation, Kitty's current predicament served as a warning. Kitty's sisters saw just how precarious life as a courtesan was, and how fleeting success could prove to be. Kitty was now all too painfully aware of this fact. Courtesans, unless they had managed to make a good marriage, generally fell by the wayside as they aged. One who had slipped into destitution was the once-notorious Lucy Cooper.

Lucy Cooper's origins remain hazy. Her mother was said to run one of London's bawdy houses, and Lucy grew up alongside the girls who worked there. As she had a natural beauty, it was no surprise that Lucy would seek out fame and fortune in the capital's seedy underbelly. Depending on which account you prefer, Lucy was either possessed of an innate elegance or, in a description which harked back to the immoral royal court a century earlier, 'lewder than all the whores in Charles' reign'. At about the same time that Kitty had become famous, Lucy found a wealthy protector in the aged – and normally frugal – Sir Orlando Bridgeman, 4th Baronet. The besotted old man paid for a house on Parliament Street in Westminster. There he housed Lucy, replete with new furniture, carriage, and servants. She lived in high style, existing for the moment and without a care in the world. When Bridgeman tired of his expensive mistress, Lucy managed to keep hold of the roof over her head… at least for a while. *Harris's List* contained an entry for Lucy in the 1761 edition, advertising the fact that she was back 'on the town'. It gave her address as Parliament Street and referred to Sir Orlando Bridgeman as Sir Penurious Trifle. Lucy, it went on to say, had 'squandered for him 14,000*l.* without realising 1,400*l.* She is closely connected with an actor at the Old House; and some people say, they have tucked themselves up in the matrimonial noose; but the theatrical legends range this article under the head of apocrypha.'[23]

Lucy hadn't bothered to plan for the future. According to the actor and theatre manager Tate Wilkinson (who was one of Lucy's friends and probably the actor mentioned above), she even threw a document which gave her a financial settlement from Sir Orlando into the fire during a row. Little surprise it was then that Lucy found herself beset by debts and chased from pillar to post by bailiffs. She moved from Parliament Street to Bath, and then back to London and a dingy house in a courtyard just off Bow Street. There, Lucy suffered a further blow when a fire broke out in a nearby coach painter's premises on Long Acre. It spread quickly and consumed several houses, hers included. After this disaster, Lucy had lost everything. She owed an eye-watering amount of money and, because of these debts, she was confined in the King's Bench Prison. There she stayed, alone and destitute for several months until a few remaining friends (Tate Wilkinson and the gossipy memoirist, William Hickey, amongst them) paid her bills and secured her freedom. It was, however, a fleeting respite. Lucy's confinement had nearly finished her off. She was ill and her looks had long gone. Lucy scraped by for another year or so until her death aged just 42. Would a future such as this also be Kitty's fate? She must have feared that she was at risk of ending in a debtors' prison. Kitty had to act fast and needed all her quick wits to relaunch herself. Her past celebrity was still something upon which she could capitalise. In London, Kitty's fame was about to get a public boost, even while she was eaten up with grief.[24]

With her precarious future in mind, Kitty had turned not to Joshua Reynolds, but to an artist who was his rival. She wanted a portrait that would re-announce her presence on the scene. The artist she chose was an Irishman, Nathaniel Hone, and he painted what has become the most iconic portrait of Kitty. Her image was always of paramount importance to Kitty. She carefully controlled it via her portraits. This one is no exception and is a masterstroke in the art of self-promotion. Having been out of the spotlight for several years, Kitty needed a way to regain the public's attention. No longer Mrs Brown the housekeeper, she had to once again be Kitty Fisher, a celebrated courtesan. It was a noted fact that a woman new to the scene was more desirable, and could command more money. Around six years had passed since Kitty's accident in the Mall, and she had been out of the public's eye for five of them. She was in her mid-twenties, not exactly an old maid but still past the first flush of her youth and with a lot of emotional baggage. Although she had to rely on all her cosmetic arts to disguise the damage to her skin from using ceruse, Kitty was still a beauty. She had to capitalise on that, and her past notoriety. In short, Kitty had to regain her celebrity status. This portrait was her way of doing that. Self-assuredly gazing out from the canvas, Kitty is every inch the *femme fatale* of old. She wears a white gown, a symbol of purity that mocks her profession. Clutched to her breast is a silken fabric, embroidered with gold thread. Kitty's hair is loosely tied back and falls nonchalantly over one shoulder. Her cheeks are rouged and her lips seductive. Strands of pearls are wrapped around her wrist. On a table next to Kitty is a glass bowl in which six goldfish swim and a black and white cat is perched on the edge, dipping his paw into the water. It is a play on her name, the kitty-cat is fishing. There is one more detail in the painting which highlights Kitty's once all-pervasive celebrity. A windowpane is reflected in the goldfish bowl, and the shadows of people clamouring to look at Kitty through that window can be seen. The painting encompasses Kitty's fame, her allure, and her sexuality.[25]

It was in May 1765 that Nathaniel Hone's portrait of Kitty was included in an exhibition by the Society of Artists of Great Britain. It took place at Christopher Cock's Auction Rooms in Spring Gardens near Charing Cross. Although titled *Portrait of a Lady*, everyone knew the painting showed Kitty. It was the highlight of the whole exhibition:

A few observations on the pictures at Spring Gardens … This is the Portrait of a Lady, *whose charms are well known to the town.* The Painter has ingeniously attempted to acquaint us with the name by a Rebus upon Canvas. By her side a *kitten* [KITTY] is attempting to get into a basin of gold *fish* [KITTY FISH] – what pity it is, he did not make the Rebus complete, and, according to Subtle in the Alchemist, place on the other side a Dog snarling – *er* – KITTY FISH – ER![26]

Any benefit Kitty derived from the reception of Hone's painting was short-lived. There were no men who offered to keep her. Then, four months after the exhibition, Kitty's father died. John Henry Fischer's funeral took place in Soho, in the churchyard attached to St Anne's and close to the house in which Kitty had been born. The pressure on Kitty increased with his death. Now she was, to all intents and purposes, the head of her family, and the family's sole breadwinner. Kitty gave up the lease on Titsey Place and came back to London. Her mother and siblings left Carrington Street and moved into Bruton Street with Kitty. Everything was now consolidated into that melancholy house, and it was up to Kitty to keep the bailiffs from the door. Two days after her father's funeral, she returned to Joshua Reynolds's studio. The one sure way that Kitty knew to make people pay attention to her was via her image. She hoped to emulate the success of Reynolds's earlier portraits of her, with copies replicated in print shops around the country. Perhaps Reynolds, her friend and rumoured former lover, suggested to Kitty that he paint her portrait again, knowing they could both benefit financially?[27]

It might be another unfinished portrait of Kitty which resulted from this sitting. As he had in the Cleopatra painting, Reynolds once again depicted Kitty in the guise of another woman. This time it was as a character from Greek mythology. Kitty was Danaë, a Princess of Argos. In the legend, it was prophesised that Danaë's father, King Acrisius, would be killed by his daughter's son. He imprisoned Danaë but Zeus appeared as a shower of gold and seduced her, leaving the princess pregnant. Their son was the hero Perseus, who did indeed kill his grandfather, by accident. In paintings of the myth, the shower of gold is often shown as gold coins and the tale has become synonymous with prostitution. Was Kitty playing on her past notoriety, knowing what a sensation the portrait would cause because of the parallels that would be drawn between it and her own life? On the canvas, Kitty rests on a couch, her gaze knowing as she once again looks directly towards the viewer. Kitty's stomach appears rounded, denoting a pregnancy, either real or imagined. A small figure peeps from behind her, maybe a dog, or a child. This painting has been described as Joshua Reynolds's 'most overly erotic picture'. Kitty was once again every inch the courtesan, rather than a contented mistress or fashionable society lady.[28]

Kitty had no choice but to pick up where she'd left off. The only option she had was to find a keeper and she needed to find one fast. She could spare no more time to grieve for Chetwynd or her father, no matter how heartbroken she might have been in private. She had to capitalise on her youth and beauty while she still could, or face ruin. Chetwynd's debts were for his family to worry about, but Kitty was struggling financially too. Any money Kitty had possessed had been spent. It turns out that, like Lucy Cooper, Kitty had failed to save enough for a rainy day. Of the men who used to vie for her attention, all but one had moved on, married, or had passed away.

Earl Poulett was dead. The Earl of Coventry was happily married to his second wife. Sir Charles Bingham had snared himself an heiress and settled down. Thomas Bromley, 2nd Baron Montfort was still single and pursuing the Italian soprano, Giulia Frasi around town. Even if he could be distracted from her, Kitty had proved too expensive for him the first time around. There were no expectations that it would be any different now. In desperation, and in the immediate aftermath of her father's death, Kitty sought out the one man who she thought might rescue her, Joseph Salvador. Though she had been indifferent to him in the early days of her career, he was now the best, perhaps the only choice available. If Salvador realised Kitty had turned to him as her last option, he didn't care. He accepted with alacrity and proved generous. In total, during the few months that he was Kitty's protector, Salvador gave her £1,575 (although a later dispute raged as to whether the money was given as a gift, or as a loan). Salvador wrote a letter to Kitty itemising some of the transactions: '£300 towards your support and your family; £100 towards mourning on your father's decease; £100 as a present on your journey to Bath and £100 for expenses on the journey; £500 as a token of my love and affection and in consideration of the many necessary expenses you must incur to appear – as I desire you.'[29]

With Salvador's money, Kitty attempted to enjoy herself and appear the desirable courtesan of a few years earlier. She was living at the centre of fashionable society once again, but her life was not as before. Kitty was older and wiser. She had experienced as much pain as happiness in her short life and now was having to make do. Although not quite yesterday's news, Kitty's celebrity did not shine as bright as it once had. In the space of seven months, she had lost two of the most important people in her life, and the year still had one last drama in store.

It was perhaps because her mother and sisters lived with her again that Kitty continued to call herself Mrs Martin. For their sake, she wanted the gloss of respectability and anonymity that the assumed name gave her. However, when the unexpected glare of public scrutiny threatened to reveal her lies, Kitty had to think on her feet. The only option was to tell yet more untruths. There had been a robbery at Kitty's home. One of her servants stole some household items and was caught trying to sell them. The whole sorry debacle ended up in the law courts and someone from Kitty's family had to take to the witness box and give evidence to the judge and jury at the trial.

Kitty's thieving servant was Charles Johnson. His light-fingers spirited away two silver tablespoons, a silver teaspoon, a china cup and saucer, and a damask napkin. Johnson left the house, hurried past Berkeley Square and onto Mount Street, where his misadventure ended in his arrest. Three weeks later, he found himself in the dock of the Old Bailey. Knowing Kitty's presence in the courtroom would result in a blaze of publicity, it was Anne Fischer, Kitty's mother, who took the stand as a witness. Anne colluded in her daughter's lies. They both knew there was a danger of the case being reported in the newspapers. Kitty didn't want her real name connected with the trial. Nor did she want Anthony George Martin to realise that, seven years after he'd abandoned her, she was still using his surname. Kitty and her mother invented a husband named Henry Martin. Anne Fischer explained her pretended son-in-law's absence from the home they shared. Henry Martin was, Mrs Fischer said, onboard a ship, sailing the high seas. The lie was almost enough to hide Kitty. In reality, Johnson had already given the game away to the man who first apprehended him. This was mentioned during the trial but escaped wider notice. Maybe the judge thought Johnson had been lying? Kitty's presence in the drama remained a secret from the world at large. The transcript of the court case has survived and proves Kitty's connection with the drama:

Lazarus Mordecai: I sell oranges and lemons. Last Wednesday was a fortnight I was in Mount-street, Grosvenor-square: I met the prisoner; he wanted to sell me two silver spoons, I said I would not buy them: he said they were not marked, I might buy them. There was Moses Manuell by, I bid him take them in his hand; he did; then I told the prisoner he should not have them again, without he would go into somebody's house with me, and bring the owner of them: we went a little way; he catched hold of the spoons and bent them. *[The spoons were held up in court, for the jury to see.]* I sent Moses for a constable: the prisoner went into a public house, and threw the spoons into the yard, where they were found; then we secured him; he at first said a fellow servant had given them to him. We took him before a Justice, he said they belonged to his mistress, that he said was Kitty Fisher; that he took them in the kitchen.

Moses Manuell: I am an old cloathsman: I met the prisoner; he asked me to buy these two spoons; I said I did not buy such; he said, get me somebody to buy them. I not being strong enough to secure him, went to this Mordecai, and gave him an account of what the prisoner had said; then he went to the prisoner. *[The rest of Moses Manuell's statement was the same as Lazarus Mordecai's]*

Anne Fisher: I am Mrs Martin's mother. The prisoner owned he took these things from her. I cannot swear to the two table spoons; we lost such: the tea spoon and other things I know very well to be her property. My daughter's husband is gone to sea; his name is Henry.

John Lewis: I am a beadle of St. George's parish; I was sent for to take the prisoner in custody: he and the things were delivered to my charge; he acknowledged he had taken these spoons to pay his passage to his mother (he was a black) he said she lived in the plantations abroad.

Robert Sherrard: I took up these table spoons in the yard where the prisoner had thrown them.

The prisoner said nothing in his defence.

Despite his crime and although he didn't speak up, the reason behind Charles Johnson's actions was one deserving of pity. Charles was the son of an enslaved woman who worked on one of the plantations in America and he simply wanted to return to find her. Without the means to do so, he had turned to robbery in desperation. We don't know how Charles came to be in London in the mid-1760s and the jurors at the Old Bailey didn't care. They were not swayed by emotion and found him guilty. In a sadly ironic twist of fate, Charles Johnson did get his passage to North America, just not in the way he wanted. Charles was held in the infamous Newgate prison before being transported overseas for a term of seven years.[30]

For Kitty, her life as a courtesan was about at its end. While it would have been to her advantage to snare a high-ranking peer, as others had done, all Kitty wanted was someone to love her. Someone who she could love in return. Having a title was no guarantee to happiness, as poor Lady Coventry had discovered. It was around this time that Joseph Salvador began to experience money worries. In due course, he would sell up in England and move to America. Kitty was 25, had reached the height of celebrity, and then stepped out of the limelight. She had loved, and lost, twice and now faced an uncertain future. Then, in a stroke of good luck, the hero of Kitty Fisher's story made his entrance.

Chapter Seven

Mrs Norris: A Gentleman's Wife

'It was added that Mr Norris is unfortunately a great dupe as
some of the wisest of men in all ages have been, to the sex, and has
such attachment to women of no character as is extraordinary.'
(Richard Waite Cox (of the Navy Office)
to the Norris family steward, William Ward, 1770)

John Norris, MP for the Cinque-Port town of Rye on the East
Sussex coastline, didn't initially appear to be any kind of hero.
Handsome, straightforward, and honest, Norris had a young
man's lack of common sense. He had been racing headlong down
a road leading to ruin, spending his inheritance before he had even
come into it, and his parents despaired of their son. Chasing after a
once-notorious courtesan renowned for her love of fine clothes and
diamonds might not, therefore, seem like the best plan for this devil-
may-care young man-about-town. In fact, for John Norris, it proved
to be a most sensible course of action. Or, at least, it would have been,
had fate not intervened.

As the eldest son, Norris stood to inherit Hemsted Park, his father's
Kentish estate situated near the village of Benenden. It had been
John's grandfather, the Irish-born Admiral Sir John Norris (known
as Foul-Weather Jack) who had bought the property in the early part
of the eighteenth century. The mansion had been inherited by his
son, also named John Norris, and Kitty's Mr Norris knew that, in due
course, the estate would one day be his. The Norris family also had
connections with Deal Castle, a formidable old fortress on the Kent
coastline. Sir John had been captain of the castle, and his namesake

grandson followed in his footsteps. It was while John junior was at Deal Castle towards the end of 1765 that he got to know a young mother, Mrs Catherine Knight, known as the 'Kentish Beauty'. Catherine had three sons, the youngest born that year, and the family lived in the small village of Ripple, just three miles away from the castle. All was not well in the Knight household, however. Catherine's argumentative and overbearing Welsh husband, Captain Henry Knight, had fought more than one duel and often sought redress in law. As well as his home in Kent, Captain Knight had an estate in Wales (Tythegston Court in the Vale of Glamorgan, complete with a Tudor manor house) and a townhouse in London. The Knights had married almost four years earlier, and the sons had followed at yearly intervals thereafter. There is nothing to suggest that Norris was anything other than a friend to Captain and Mrs Knight. At any rate, when he left Deal, John travelled solo to London. There, he fell into Kitty Fisher's orbit.[1]

John Norris was just the type of man Kitty had been waiting for. Importantly, he was unmarried. For Kitty, her profession had never been more than a means to an end, and all she'd ever really wanted was to be a wife and, perhaps, a mother. Kitty's heart had been stolen twice, and both times it had ended in disaster and heartbreak. Since then, she had tried to be steely in her dealings with men. Until, that is, John Norris claimed her attention. Handsome and full of the energy of youth (he was a year older than Kitty), John Norris was different to the rakes and old roués who had made a play for her. He didn't just want to be Kitty's keeper, he fell in love with her. Kitty never did need much encouragement to follow suit. She allowed herself to lose her heart for the third time and returned Norris's affection tenfold. Anne Fischer gave her seal of approval to her daughter's new lover, but John Norris's parents were not amused in the slightest at the turn of events. Already despairing of their scapegrace son running through his fortune, they now had to watch him set up home with a scandalous 'lady of the town'. They hoped and prayed that Norris's love affair with Kitty would be short-lived and issued vague threats about disinheritance if he allowed things to go too far.

The house on Bruton Street where Kitty lived with her mother and sisters was soon full of excitement. Over the following twelve months, there would be not one, not two, but three weddings. Kitty's youngest sister, 18-year-old Sarah Louisa, was the first to marry. She walked down the aisle of St George's in Hanover Square on a bright spring day to wed John Pollard, a brewer from Soho. The couple set up home in Marylebone and, within weeks, a baby was on the way. In the past, Kitty had used her money to set up old friends and neighbours with apprenticeships and jobs and tried to match-make between them. Perhaps Kitty had brought about her sister's marriage, determined that Sarah would have some security? If so, maybe she remembered the proposal she had received from the pewterer's son while she was still in her teens. While she had walked one path through life, Kitty didn't want that for her sister. For Sarah, a respectable marriage to a tradesman was welcomed with open arms by the Fischer family. However, the new Mrs Pollard's departure from Bruton Street left a gap in the little household.[2]

Just as her life seemed to be settling on an even keel, Kitty was horrified to discover that her old enemy, Jack Harris, was about to traduce her in print. Five years earlier, Kitty had been mentioned in *Harris's List*, the directory which bore his name but which otherwise was nothing to do with him. Now, Jack Harris decided to try his hand at writing and publishing a rival directory. He couldn't name it after himself, so he chose the name of a woman known only too well to the men of London. *Kitty's Attalantis* was published in early 1766. It was not a success. Harris did not have the clever wit that Samuel Derrick had brought to *Harris's List*, and his version was second-rate. It was most certainly not the sort of publication that Kitty wanted to see her name connected with. As well as the title referencing her, Kitty is more than likely alluded to on the second page of this pseudo-*Harris's List*. 'The smart Mrs F___r, little and pretty, rather too much dress, very fond of a side box at the playhouse; in keeping with a noble lord, in an honour'd court. – *Pall-mall.*' John Norris had taken the lease on an impressive white stuccoed townhouse on King Street in Piccadilly. It was an upmarket street that ran parallel to Pall Mall and opened out onto St James's Square. Kitty had wasted no time and moved in with him, as Jack Harris knew. Her widowed mother moved back to Soho, safe in the knowledge that two of her daughters now looked settled and were being cared for.[3]

While Kitty's prospects were looking up, her old friend Jane Skrine, née Sumner, had not been so lucky. She had become ill and travelled to Rome, where she died less than two years after her marriage. Horace Walpole was in Paris at the time and as soon as he heard the news he wrote to his friend, Horace Mann, remarking that Skrine would be 'glad of his consort's departure. She was a common creature, bestowed on the public by Lord Sandwich.' Jane left her daughter, Louisa, in the care of William Skrine, but only while he remained unmarried. In the event he made a second marriage, Jane directed that her brother, William Brightwell Sumner, be Louisa's guardian instead. In the space of just a few years, Kitty's world had changed dramatically but she still hoped for a happy ending to her own life. It appeared to be within sight.[4]

At the end of September, Kitty once again visited Joshua Reynolds's studio. The portrait of her as Danaë was still unfinished, destined to remain so. It was probably to Kitty's relief. Where she had once tried to recapture her status as a 'celebrated courtesan', now she wanted to appear respectable. The painting she was sitting for perhaps had greater personal importance. It could be that it was intended to mark an important new beginning in Kitty's life. The event that Mr and Mrs Norris feared most was about to become reality. Kitty's latest portrait may have been intended to commemorate her wedding. The Pollards' happiness in married life proved infectious. Despite his parents' warnings, John Norris asked Kitty to become his wife. She didn't hesitate and accepted him straight away. They just had to work out how to get the ceremony performed without the knowledge of John's parents, who were threatening to put a halt to proceedings. Kitty's family were on side and a plan was hatched. The two lovers travelled north and crossed the border into Scotland. They had taken Kitty's new brother-in-law, John Pollard, with them, in their coach. The journey, in the late autumn, was a long and arduous one, and Sarah, heavily pregnant, stayed behind in London. The threesome headed for the small town of Haddington in East Lothian.[5]

Since 1754, so-called 'irregular' marriages were illegal in England. No longer was it possible to make a clandestine marriage in front of two witnesses, often strangers to the bride and groom. Now, a licence had to be procured or banns published for four consecutive weeks before the ceremony was performed. This gave the public notice of the wedding and – if there was an objection to it taking place – a chance to make sure it didn't happen. John Norris didn't want to give his parents a chance to object. In Scotland, no such restrictions applied and there was a constant stream of couples who eloped north of the border to say their vows. The famous blacksmith's shop at Gretna Green was a favourite venue, as was the toll house on Coldstream Bridge. Haddington's Presbyterian Church conducted marriages in a religious setting but without the need for banns nor a licence. All that was required were two witnesses. On 25 October 1766, a Saturday, John Norris and Kitty Fisher stood in front of Haddington's minister to say their vows. John Pollard was by their side to act as a witness, together with Bartholomew Bower, a local man who acted as a spare witness at many weddings. Bower was the church's precentor and a former Jacobite rebel who had supported Bonnie Prince Charlie in the 1745 uprising. Kitty and John left Haddington as man and wife.[6]

Back in London, when the marriage became known, the Norris family mounted a challenge. They tried to have the union declared invalid and wanted nothing to do with their new daughter-in-law. The deed was done, however, and news of the match spread like wildfire. The newspapers told how, 'The celebrated Miss Kitty Fisher has, within these few days, been married to ___ N___, Esq; a gentleman of considerable family and fortune.' Had John Henry Fischer lived a little longer, he would have been proud of his daughter. Kitty had achieved just what he had hoped for, a marriage that was a love match to a gentleman of fortune who would one day own a fine estate. Mr and Mrs Norris were not so pleased with their renegade son. The furore caused by their anger ignited gossip and speculation. It was suggested that the marriage, carried out so secretly, was indeed null and void. To silence both the rumours and the Norris family, there was nothing else for it. Kitty and John had to marry for a second time, with all conventions adhered to. John went to the Vicar General's office to get a marriage licence which let the couple marry straight away. Two days later, on a crisp and cold December day, Kitty and John turned up at St George's in Hanover Square. With little fanfare or celebration, they went through their vows to one another again and, in an echo of that first marriage, John Pollard once more stood as a witness. The marriage entry in the parish register bears testament to the confusion: 'John Norris, Esq., bachelor and Catherine Maria Norris, heretofore Fischer, both of this parish, were married in this church…' They were one of six couples who married at St George's on that day. Their second witness was a woman named Sarah Cawthorn, who performed the same function for two of the other couples. Sarah appeared regularly in the parish registers, fulfilling the position of a witness for those who had no one else to ask. It suggests that Kitty and John married with few friends and family present besides John Pollard. It may have just been the three of them who made up the small wedding party, as was the case for the Scottish ceremony. The Fischer family's joy at Kitty becoming Mrs Norris was short-lived, however. Two weeks after Kitty's second wedding, Sarah Louisa Pollard died in childbirth. She was just 19 years old. Her baby was stillborn.[7]

Kitty and John left London and travelled down to Kent to stay at his family's estate, Hemsted Park in the village of Benenden.

Their quiet honeymoon, taken so soon after Sarah Louisa's death, spanned the Christmas period. Maybe Kitty's grief encouraged John's parents to sympathise with their new daughter-in-law? Once they had got to know the woman behind the celebrity, all their doubts faded. Far from leading John astray, Kitty was a good influence. She curbed John's impetuosity and her new in-laws appreciated the fact that Kitty calmed her husband's wild streak. To their surprise, they discovered that Kitty Fisher was one person and Mrs Catherine Maria Norris another altogether. While at Benenden, Kitty was happy to get to know the people who lived and worked at the house and in the surrounding area. Still a keen horsewoman, despite the cold weather she was often out riding with her husband. When they passed someone, Kitty always stopped to talk. She expected that one day, she would be the 'lady of the manor', and started as she meant to go on. As Kitty chatted with Benenden's tenants and labourers, her natural charm shone through. She was soon loved by all. The Norris family celebrated the New Year with high hopes for the future. It was a new beginning, one filled with love, with dreams, and with hope. It was the life Kitty had always wanted.[8]

John Norris didn't trouble parliament too often in his capacity as an MP, but when he did, he sat on the Duke of Newcastle's interest. He was always a good friend to his patron, voting as Newcastle wanted. Towards the end of February, John sent his apologies rather than travel to London to attend a division on land tax. He excused himself, saying that it was 'private family business' which prevented his attendance. Perhaps his friends laughed, and speculated that Kitty Fisher's charms were more interesting than dull parliamentary procedure? If only that had been the case. The truth is that something was wrong.

That seems like an understatement. In reality, everything was as wrong as wrong could be. Kitty, just 25, was dying. Simon Trusty, in his printed attack on Kitty seven years earlier, had proved prophetic. He had warned her, 'Be wife, then, before it is too late;

your triumphant Days will be short; Beauty is a perishable Thing; Sickness may take the Coral from your Lip, the Tincture from your Cheek, the Fire from your Eye…' Kitty had waited too long to be a wife and now it was, indeed, too late for her. There would be no children, no years as the mistress of Hemsted Park, no long and happy life as Mrs Norris.

Kitty had nursed William Chetwynd through his fatal illness. It seems that Kitty's care for him contributed to her death. It is a cruel irony that for Kitty, the era's most 'celebrated courtesan', her loving heart proved to be her unwitting downfall. Kitty had unknowingly contracted tuberculosis from Chetwynd. It was a disease that took some time to show itself. When it did, like Maria Gunning before her, Kitty's immune system mounted no defence. It had been fatally weakened by her use of lead-based skin-whitening make-up. For a few weeks, Kitty put her ailments down to other causes. Maybe her cough was a winter cold? Slowly, realisation dawned. When the disease became apparent, it progressed with a speed that took everyone by surprise. Kitty must have known that there was little hope of recovery. The deaths in her past, those of William Chetwynd, of Maria, Countess of Coventry, and the Henderson boy, would all have played on her mind.

A pen and ink miniature by Richard Cosway dating to this period replicates Kitty as she was painted by Reynolds with the two doves. However, Kitty and the doves are placed in a classical garden that is full of symbolism. A Grecian urn stands behind Kitty, and in front is a birdbath. In the background, a large mansion can be glimpsed. It's tempting to think that this is an imagined scene in Hemsted Park's grounds. Behind Kitty are two trees, one flowering and one dead. Honeysuckle and roses represent fertility, perhaps a wished-for child. This symbolism seems especially pertinent if we consider that the drawing was executed around the time of Kitty's illness. The reference to fertility is interesting. Nowhere in Kitty's history has it been suggested that she ever fell pregnant. Could this indicate a final tragic element to her early death? Was Kitty in the early stages of pregnancy when she fell ill? Or did she initially ascribe any queasiness to symptoms of pregnancy, thinking she had morning sickness?[9]

By March, hope was running out. Kitty and John Norris headed for Bristol's Hotwells to 'take the waters'. They hoped for a miracle. The winter had been severe and the journey was slow going, managed in stages along treacherous, icy roads. They made a stop at the Castle Inn in Marlborough, a popular resting place for travellers heading towards the southwest. There is a tantalising reference to a relic from this stop. In the early twentieth century, a gentleman in New York whose family was from England claimed to have a piece of window glass from the Castle Inn. On this fragment of glass was etched – perhaps with one of Kitty's favourite diamonds – her name and the date: 'Kitty Fisher, 1767'. The Castle Inn was later part of Marlborough College and the gentleman's father had worked there, found the piece of glass, and kept it. Did Kitty want to confirm her presence in life, while on her journey to death? Did she – or her husband – scratch the name by which she was known to the world into the window of her room, a defiant act of graffiti to record the fact that Kitty Fisher still lived?[10]

On Monday, 9 March the Norrises' carriage rolled into Bath. They planned their stay to be just one more stop on their road to Bristol. Approaching the King's Bath, they drove into Abbeygate Street and then turned into a 6ft passage which led into the large and busy stable yard of the Three Tuns Inn on Stall Street. It was a hostelry kept by a local man, the well-connected Henry Phillott. Behind the inn was the Three Tuns lodging house, where rooms could be taken for the night. Outside, people went about their daily business, unaware that the century's biggest celebrity was so close by. Nor were they aware that the final act of Kitty's dramatic life was about to unfold on their very doorstep.

Instead, the people of Bath goggled at the 'Grand Collection of China' which was being exhibited two doors down at the Green Tree House run by Mrs Dart. Here, they could buy Persian carpets, blue and white patterned plates, and Mandarin figurines. Two houses along from the Pump Room passage and up one set of stairs was a haberdashery, Atkins and Lyne. They sold fabrics of all descriptions, silks, sarcenets, flowered satins, striped damasks, and printed cotton alongside silk stockings, ribbons, and handkerchiefs. John Sowerby, a woollen-draper who also sold headwear and hosiery, had a shop near the Three Tuns. Equestriennes could visit his shop to buy white-furred and plain black riding hats, and coloured feathers to trim them with. Numerous coffee houses competed for business, and sedan chairmen touted for hire.

The major attraction on Stall Street, though, was the King's and Queen's Baths. The old Roman baths were filled with hot spring water which was thought to have healing properties. In Kitty's day, it was still possible to bathe in them and the Three Tuns lodging house overlooked this scene. For more refined visitors and invalids, there was the Pump Room, just around the corner on Abbey Church Yard. It had opened some sixty years earlier, and there ladies and gentlemen who didn't want to bathe could drink the spring water. From the Pump Room's veranda, guests sat and watch the bathers in the King's Bath when the weather was warm enough.[11]

For cities such as Bath, the winter months were 'out of season'. With parliament in session, the *haut ton* congregated in London. In the capital, they could enjoy all the entertainments on offer while the men who were lords and MPs were within easy reach of the Houses of Parliament. Therefore, Bath was much quieter than it was during the busy summertime. The majority of visitors to the city during the colder months were invalids with their families and attendants. They were all there with one aim: to drink or bathe in the spring water that was supposed to cure a range of ailments. Even in its off-season, though, Bath still ran to a strict timetable. This had been enforced by an earlier Master of Ceremonies, Beau Nash (Fanny Murray's lover), who set the rules for everything. These included the time of the last dance in the ballroom (11.00 pm on the dot) and what could, and could not, be worn. On a normal day, the Bath timetable began with bathing followed by a visit to the Pump Room for three glasses of Bath's water. If the weather was dismal, the afternoon might be spent playing cards in the Assembly Rooms or perhaps eating Bath cakes in a tearoom. On two nights each week, if there were enough people to make it worthwhile, there was a ball in the Assembly Rooms. Day-to-day life in the city was so regimented that Elizabeth Montagu, the famous bluestocking, wrote that 'the only thing one can do today, we did not do the day before is to die; not that I would be hurried, by a love of variety and novelty, to do so irreparable a thing as dying'.[12]

If she had been well enough, Kitty would have wrapped up warm to go shopping and then visit the Pump Room for a glass of water. She might even have visited her old acquaintance, Samuel Derrick, who was Beau Nash's successor as Bath's Master of Ceremonies. There was no chance of her venturing out on this occasion, however. Kitty paid no attention to the hustle and bustle around her. Ashen-faced and weak, she was helped from her carriage where she sat bundled in blankets and furs. The inn's servants helped John carry Kitty to a bedroom in the lodging house attached to the inn. That room was to be her final destination. It was the last stop on Kitty's journey, both to the Bristol Hotwells and through life. The next morning, John discovered his wife lying speechless. Within a few hours, Kitty had done the one thing in Bath that you could do differently from the day before. In the corridors of the Pump Room, in the coffee houses and on the streets of Bath, people whispered the shocking news. The celebrated Kitty Fisher was dead.

In at least some of the newspapers, Kitty was granted the respectability she had craved for so long. The *St James's Chronicle*, for one, reported her death with no allusion to her history and notoriety. 'Died. Tuesday, at Bath, in her Way to Bristol, Mrs Norris, jun., Lady of John Norris, jun. Esq., Member of Parliament for Rye in Sussex.' John took his wife's body back to Hemsted Park. She was laid to rest in the Norris family vault at Benenden church. Knowing full well

Kitty's love of fashion and finery in life, John insisted that his wife was buried wearing her best ball gown. Two months later, he visited Kitty's old friend, Joshua Reynolds. There are three sittings recorded for Norris. If Reynolds had been painting a picture of Kitty to mark her new beginning as a wife, no doubt John would have wanted a companion portrait. Now, after Kitty's death, those portraits would be a lasting memento of his short-lived happiness. Nothing has survived to say if these paintings were finished or, if they were, what happened to them. Events were about to overtake John Norris which might well have put all thoughts of portraits out of his mind.[13]

Chapter Eight

The Aftermath

'… the deponent once or twice, went into the dining-room to wait upon the said John Norris, and Catherine Knight … when he found them sitting together upon a settee, or couch, in a very loving posture, with the legs of one of them across the legs of the other…'

(The Deposition of James Davies, 8th June 1770 in the case of Henry Knight, Esq. against Catherine Knight)

John Norris was heartbroken. There was more to come. Eight months after Kitty's death, her father-in-law joined her in the family vault at Benenden church. If Kitty had lived just a little longer, she would have been Hemsted Park's mistress. John's mother and sister lived at Hemsted and though he was now the nominal master of the estate, he found no pleasure in the fact. In his grief, he turned to old friends and spent time with Henry and Catherine Knight. The Knights had a London townhouse on Welbeck Street, close to Cavendish Square and Norris stayed with them for a time. As well as her three young sons, Catherine now had an infant daughter too. Even so, she found time to comfort John.[1]

Early the next year, Henry Knight left London for Wales. He wanted to be at his estate for the coming election. Catherine stayed behind in London. It was a year since Kitty had died. On 10 April, Knight received a letter from Catherine, begging that he would allow them to separate. Shocked, he rushed back to the capital, but it was too late. Catherine had left Welbeck Street. A furious search led Knight down to Kent. He found Catherine in Canterbury, where she had taken refuge with her family. He pleaded, cajoled, and threatened, but she refused to return to her marital home. John Norris's involvement in this family drama remains clouded. What is certain is that nine months later, Catherine was back in London. She found lodgings in a house on the corner of Charles Street, Grosvenor Square, and was often to be seen out riding with Norris. In the summer, Catherine, visibly pregnant, moved again, to a furnished house on Ham Common. John Norris remained a frequent visitor.[2]

Catherine's escape from her domineering husband, and her affair with Norris, passed under the radar of society's prying eyes. Hoping to keep her pregnancy a secret, around the end of October, Catherine returned to London from Ham Common. She took lodgings in a house in Park Street, off Grosvenor Square. Calling herself Mrs Johnson, she allowed John Norris to introduce himself to their new servants as Mr Johnson. They passed as husband and wife and in mid-November, Catherine gave birth to Norris's daughter. Six weeks later, the couple packed up, quit their rooms, and returned to Ham Common.[3]

Henry Knight was incandescent with rage when he heard the news. He found Norris and confronted him, offering him a choice. Norris could either meet Knight to fight a duel or give the captain proof of Catherine's infidelity so he could divorce her. Both routes led to disaster, but it was the latter option that Norris chose. Captain Knight instantly launched legal proceedings against Norris, known as a criminal conversation (or crim. con.) case. A wife was her husband's property, and Captain Henry Knight claimed damages for the loss of her. A full divorce allowing both parties to remarry could only be obtained via a parliamentary bill. The crueller option of legal separation was a distinct possibility, leaving no prospect of remarriage.

The case lasted several days while a procession of witnesses appeared to give damning evidence against Mrs Catherine Knight. Her servants and doctors all testified to her intimacy with Norris and recounted how they lived as man and wife under assumed names.

Catherine's maid told how she had seen the couple in bed together on more than one occasion when she came to attend to her mistress in the mornings. In the end, Captain Knight was awarded damages against John Norris of £3,000. It was a sum that all but bankrupted Kitty's widower. John Norris found himself beset on all sides. Joseph Salvador also began a court case to recover the money he had given to Kitty years earlier. Norris produced the letter Salvador had written to Kitty detailing the amounts, arguing that it had been a gift, not a loan.

It was now three years since Kitty's death, and Norris faced an uncertain future. Captain Knight pressed for a full divorce from Catherine, which was granted. She was allowed to marry again and so, as soon as she was free to do so, Catherine became the second Mrs Norris. However, for John, this union was no replica of his happy but short time with Kitty. His marriage to Catherine was a disaster, both financially and personally. Catherine's youngest son with Henry Knight had died before she married John Norris. Legally, Captain Knight had control of his other three children. Catherine was probably completely isolated from them and ran half-mad as a result. Even her daughter by Norris could have been claimed by her former husband if he wished to inflict further cruelty. Any children born to Catherine while her first marriage was intact were classed as Captain Knight's in the eyes of the law, regardless of who the father was. Only one or two people were aware, while the trial was ongoing, of an event that Captain Knight took the utmost care to keep secret. In Lambeth, a boy named Henry Hobbeson was christened but, on the corresponding entry in the parish register, no parents were named. This lad had been fathered by Captain Knight on one of his servants, a woman named Anne Hobbes. Young Henry was placed in the care of a nurse, somewhere in Lambeth.[4]

Catherine did bear at least one further child to John after their marriage, a son named John Francis Norris. Things were not happy, however. John and Catherine argued all the time and blamed one another for the catastrophic ruin they had each suffered. All too soon, the couple separated. Catherine travelled to France and there she stayed. Even though Captain Henry Knight had, by this time, died, Catherine still didn't regain the children she had borne him. Knight had directed that his aunt, a woman named Anne Basset, should have the care of them. John's luck was no better. Creditors were chasing him from pillar to post. He sold much of his estate apart from the mansion house itself. His mother lived there, tenant of the house for the duration of her life, and he could do nothing about it. After Mrs Norris died in 1780, John had no option but to sell Hemsted Park. The following year, his estranged wife passed away at Chatou near Paris. John Norris was a widower once more, but this time he had two children to take care of. All his parents' fears had become reality. He was ruined and his inheritance lost, but it was not Kitty who had been the cause, except by her absence from John's life.

A broken man, John Norris lived out his days in obscurity. He had a house in scenic, semi-rural surroundings on the outskirts of London, at 25 Penton Street, Pentonville. Still beset by debts despite selling his ancestral home, John scrimped, saved, begged, and borrowed to pay for his son to attend a decent school. Whenever they could, John, together with his children, left the city for the open Kentish countryside and his sister's home in the village of East Malling. It was at his sister's home that John Norris died, aged 71, in 1811. His burial did not take place there, however. His body was carried back to the church at Benenden. There, John was laid to rest beside the woman who had been his one true love, Kitty Fisher.[5]

Chapter Nine

Lucy Locket Lost Her Pocket

'Lucy Locket lost her pocket,
Kitty Fisher found it;
Not a penny was there in it,
Only ribbon round it.'

Kitty Fisher's name is today synonymous with a popular nursery rhyme. First noted many years after her death, there is that one contemporary allusion to Kitty's name in connection with that of Lucy Locket, or rather Lockit, as mentioned in an earlier chapter. In *The Meretriciad*, the author said that:

Thy man's a bankrupt both in purse and lust;
And tho' the Sun shines, yet may fortune frown,
And quite reduce, both him, and Mrs Brown.
Mankind's deceitful, you have had your swing,
Remember L__k_t wore a brilliant ring.
Kitty repent, a settlement procure,
Retire, and keep the Bailiffs from the door,
Too well thou'rt known, too long you've play'd the whore,
Put up with wrinkles, and pray paint no more:
No more thou'rt thought a subject for the Town,
Reject Miss Kitty, for plain Mrs Brown.

The Meretriciad plays with the personas of Lucy Lockit and Polly Peachum from *The Beggar's Opera*. It may be that the nursery rhyme derives from this. Also in *The Meretriciad*, Polly Davis's catfight with

Kitty at Ranelagh Gardens was recounted. Polly had lost William Chetwynd to Kitty's greater charms. Perhaps Lucy Locket represents Polly and, if so, the 'purse' she lost was William Chetwynd's, such as it was, for he was never reckoned to be too plump in his pockets. Kitty Fisher, meanwhile, had 'found' Chetwynd's purse but realised there was little of any use in it. Instead of enjoying the high life, Chetwynd spirited Kitty away into the tumbledown Titsey Place, and then left her nearly destitute when he died a few years later.

However, by the time that the nursery rhyme began to gain traction, the Honourable William Richard Chetwynd and Polly Davis were long forgotten. Perhaps all that remained was the faint memory of Kitty's connection with Lucy Lockit in *The Meretriciad*? Instead, in the popular imagination, Lucy may have taken on the persona of Lucy Cooper, one of Kitty's rival courtesans. In truth, Lucy Locket might well be an amalgam of any one or all of those high priestesses of the *demimonde* who enjoyed their fame around the same time as Kitty Fisher. She might represent Lucy Cooper, Fanny Murray, Nancy Parsons, Polly Davis, or Nelly O'Brien.

In the late 1760s, a year after Kitty's death, a thief – and possibly prostitute too – named Louisa Smith used the alias Lucy Locket. Louisa had been accused of stealing silver buckles and other items from a man named Samuel Sutton. He had been found at St Bartholomew Fair, drunk, by Louisa who offered him the use of her bed in her lodging at Black Boy Alley off Chick Lane in Smithfield. Sutton claimed that when he awoke, Louisa was gone and so were his belongings. That time, Louisa was acquitted. She was not so lucky when, a few months later, together with her friend, Mary Harris, Louisa found herself before the judge again. She was found guilty, this time of robbing a purse (containing ten guineas and one penny) belonging to a countryman visiting London. Benjamin Shotten, a horse dealer from Wolverhampton in Staffordshire, had been lured to a bawdy house run by Ann Wilder. It was in the notorious Black Boy Alley. There, Shotten claimed to have been robbed and assaulted so badly he thought he was going to be murdered. Louisa and Mary were found guilty, sentenced to hang, and thrown into Newgate to await their fate. The following year, their death sentences were commuted to transportation for life, and both women were shipped overseas. Whether or not he had been their victim, Benjamin Shotten was no better than they. In 1772, he found himself in the dock together with other members of a gang who pretended to be countrymen and horse dealers but who were swindlers. Shotten, it was discovered, had been sentenced to transportation following a crime in Lichfield, Staffordshire, eighteen years earlier.[1]

Within Kitty's lifetime, a fruit-seller and occasional thief, Kitty Clarke, used the name of Kitty Fisher as an alias. This was when Kitty was living at Titsey Place as Mrs Brown. Perhaps, with the physical absence of the real Kitty from London, Kitty Clarke traded on the similarity in their names and maybe their looks too, and persuaded gullible men to part with their coin to have her? With women from a poor and criminal background adopting these names as pseudonyms, the rhyme may be expanded to encompass them, as well as the array of courtesans who lived in the mid-eighteenth century.[2]

The pocket in the rhyme could refer to a gentleman's purse, such as that lost by Benjamin Shotten and by extension, therefore, a man's overall wealth. It is, perhaps, reminiscent of the tale concerning Kitty and the gentleman who employed Jack Harris to bring her to him. That man forced a purse onto Kitty which she discovered in her pocket when she ran back home. However, it may also mean just what it says: a pocket. In the eighteenth century, a woman's pockets were a separate garment, worn under a petticoat. The two pockets hung loosely down either side of the legs and were attached to a ribbon tied around the waist. The voluminous skirts and petticoats worn over the top of the pockets would have an opening in the sides, through which the wearer could reach through into her pockets. In an age when women tended not to carry bags, their pockets would comfortably and conveniently store no end of essential items. They could contain money, a pocketbook, needles, scissors, keys, etc., without spoiling the lines of their dresses, especially as the gowns were often layered over hoops and panniers. An extra benefit to these pockets was added security from pickpockets, although it wasn't unknown for them to be rifled through while a woman's attention was distracted elsewhere. An early newspaper report illustrates this, one which also references a prostitute losing the item:

On Saturday Night last, a Woman was knockt down in Whitcomb Street near Leicester Square, and her Pocket cut off, wherein was 24 Shillings. Much about the same Time, and near that Place, a Nymph of the Hundreds of Drury [Lane] was attack'd and lost her Pocket, but as she had met with no Game that Night the Loss was not great, the whole amounting to no more than 5 Farthings.[3]

The rhyme is traditionally sung to the tune now known as 'Yankee Doodle Dandy' which is, it is believed, repurposed from an old folk melody. Its origins are obscure, but it is believed to date from around 1758, during the Seven Years' War. A year later, after Kitty had burst onto the scene, a version was doing the rounds titled 'Kitty Fisher's Jig'. The was the song that Horace Walpole repurposed with new lyrics, to lampoon Maria, Countess of Coventry being attacked in Hyde Park, when she was mistaken for Kitty Fisher. Almost two decades later, the ditty was sung derisively by the British forces towards the Americans during the War of Independence. New verses appeared, omitting Kitty Fisher and Lucy Locket but introducing new characters. In 1775, the following verse referenced Joseph Warren, who died at the Battle of Bunker Hill:

Dolly Bushel let a fart,
Jenny Jones she found it,
Ambrose carried to the mill,
Where Doctor Warren ground it.[4]

However, the American soldiers took the song as one of their own and changed the lyrics to the patriotic ones we know today. A decade later, 'Yankee Doodle' had morphed into yet another version, titled 'American Ballad'. It was one of the songs in a pantomime performed at Covent Garden, 'The Enchanted Castle':

Boston is a yankee town, so is Philadelphia,
You shall have a sugar-dram, and I'll have one myself.
Yakee doodle, doodle doo, yankee doodle dandy,
High doodle, doodle doo, yankee doodle dandy.
Jenny Locket lost her pocket, Sukey Sweetlips found it,
Devil a thing was in the pocket, but the border round it.
Yankee doodle, &c.
First I bought a porridge-pot, then I bought a ladle,
Then my wife was brought to bed, and now I rock the cradle.
Yankee doodle, &c.
Boston is a silly town, and if I'd my desire,
First I'd knock the Rulers down, and then I'd kick the Crier.
Yankee doodle, &c.[5]

It becomes obvious, then, that there were once many different verses all set to the familiar tune. However, besides the now traditional version of Yankee Doodle 'a'riding on a pony', the only other to have endured in popular memory to this day is the verse mentioning Kitty Fisher finding Lucy Locket's pocket. It may be that Kitty's continued celebrity, via the many portraits of her, helped to retain the recognition of her name, as the ditty became the popular nursery rhyme that has been sung by children for generations.

Notes

Introduction
1. *A Collection of Songs: With Some Originals* (Dublin, 1769).

Chapter 1
1. Shaftesbury Avenue now runs where King Street once was but, when the Fischer family lived there, the street was decent and respectable, although narrower than the neighbouring ones. Kitty's date of birth is given in the old-style date. If corrected for the new style, it would be 12 June 1741. The (old-style) dates for the family are as follows, with the wedding and christenings all taking place at St Anne's, Soho: marriage of John Henry Fischer to Ann Bagnell, both 'of this parish', 26 December 1738; Catherine Maria born 1 June 1741 (christened simply as Catherine, 10 June), Ann born 22 July 1743 (christened 5 August), another daughter named Anne born 8 July 1745 (christened 17 July), Sarah Louisa born 16 November 1747 (christened as Sarah, 29 November), and lastly a son, John Henry born 3 August 1750 (christened 22 August). George II ascended the throne 11 June 1727. St Anne's church in Soho was still relatively new as it was consecrated in 1686. A silver chaser worked on the front of the piece, sinking his design into the metal (the opposite, repoussé, was the art of hammering from the reverse to produce a raised pattern on the front).
2. An apprenticeship record survives, dated 1 August 1741 (exactly two calendar months after Kitty's birth), binding John, son of Cornelius Woldring, as an apprentice to John Henry Fischer of St Anne's, a chasser [sic].
3. *The Gentlewoman's Companion: or, A Guide to the Female Sex* by Hannah Woolley, 1675. Hannah Woolley's instructions were: 'If you would prevent this slothful disease, be sure you let not those under your command to want imployment, that will hinder the growth of this distemper, and cure a worser Malady of a love-sick breast, for business will not give them time to think of such idle matters. But if this Green-sickness hath already got footing in the body, use this means to drive it away: Take a quart of Claret-wine, one pound of curran[t]s, and a handful of Rosemary-tops, with half an ounce of Mace, seeth these to a pint, and let the Patient drink thereof three spoonfuls at a time, Morning and Evening, and eat some of the Curran[t]s after.' While *The Juvenile Adventures of Miss Kitty Fisher* (London, 1759) talks about Kitty having the 'green sickness' upon her return home from boarding school, the author doesn't mention she stayed in Paddington, nor Kitty nursing John Henderson's brother at his death.

The fact that John Henderson recalled this episode and places Kitty there at the same age does corroborate the fact that she was indeed unwell in her mid-teens.

4. *The Juvenile Adventures of Miss Kitty Fisher* (London, 1759).

5. *Memoirs of the celebrated Miss Fanny Murray: Interspersed with the intrigues and amours of several eminent personages. Founded on real facts* (Dublin, 1759). *The Covent Garden Ladies: Pimp General Jack and the Extraordinary Story of Harris's List* (Tempus, 2005) by Hallie Rubenhold. Kitty Fisher was mentioned in the 1761 *Harris's List*. As that is the earliest edition to have survived, we cannot know if she appeared in an earlier one.

6. *The London Tradesman, Being a Compendious View of All the Trades, Professions, Arts, Both Liberal and Mechanic, Now Practised in the Cities of London and Westminster. Calculated for the Information of Parents, and Instruction of Youth in Their Choice of Business*, by R. Campbell, Esq. (London, 1747)

7. *Memoirs of a Woman of Pleasure* (London, 1749) by John Cleland.

8. Dorothy's father was Hammond Clement, postmaster at Darlington, Co. Durham. The clergyman's wife who discovered her was Catherine Secker, née Benson, wife of Thomas Secker, later Archbishop of Canterbury. Mrs Secker's words quoted from *The Piozzi Letters: 1805–1810*, Volume 4 (University of Delaware Press, 1996). Robert Walpole (1676–1745) was the first head of government to be known by the unofficial title of prime minister.

9. Extract from *The Juvenile Adventures of Miss Kitty Fisher* (London, 1759). Information on Mrs White from 'Histories of the Tête-à-tête annex'd (No. 19, 20) Honoris and Mrs Wh__te' in *The Town and Country Magazine or Universal Repository of Knowledge, Instruction, and Entertainment* for July 1769. Mrs White reputedly went on to snare Hugh Percy, 1st Duke of Northumberland. Anthony George Martin was christened on 27 January 1730 at the British Factory Chaplaincy in Lisbon, Portugal, his parents named on the record as 'Anth. Martyn and Martha'. Panton's Square linked Coventry Street with Great Windmill Street (via Panton Stables) and was later known as Arundel Street. It is now demolished. Martin is recorded at that address in 1755, on a Court of Chancery pleading held by The National Archives (hereinafter NA), Martin v Southern, C 11/2201/12.

10. Information on Polly Armstrong from the 1761 edition of *Harris's List*, via *Harris's List of Covent Garden Ladies: Sex in the City in Georgian Britain* (Tempus, 2005) by Hallie Rubenhold.

11. The *Gentleman's Magazine*, 1800. Anthony Martin's will (NA PROB 11/1342/71, 8 May 1800) named no children.

Chapter 2

1. Kitty's house is long gone. Norfolk Street is now known as Dunraven Street, and when the street changed name it was no. 26. Now the site is occupied by an apartment block known as Avenfield House.

2. Unfortunately, it seems that Bet's biographical verse, in which she called herself Cassandra, never saw the light of day; certainly, no record of it has yet come to light.

3. Bet Flint's trial took place at the Old Bailey on 13 September 1758. Dr Johnson told the tale of Bet bringing Kitty to his house to his friend Fanny Burney, Madame D'Arblay who recorded it in her memoirs. Meard Street (between Wardour and Dean Streets and which connected Meard's Court with Dean's Court) survives; the house in which Bet Flint lived is now known as 9 Meard Street. A Captain Baldwin (no other name given) is listed as the owner of a house in Meard's Court for 1758 and 1759 in the Westminster Rate Books; he appears to be in arrears, which supports Mary Walthow's assertion that he was abroad and she didn't know whether he was dead or alive. The 67th Regiment of Foot had been the second battalion of the 20th Foot, but in 1758 was renumbered and made a regiment in its own right. Captain John Baldwin did return to England and by the late spring of 1760 was leading a regimental recruiting party (*Whitehall Evening Post*, 29–31 May 1760). The Chief Justice was William Murray, Baron (later 1st Earl of) Mansfield.

4. The *London Chronicle*, 28–30 April 1763, said that 'A few days since died the celebrated Bett Beuley, late companion to Kitty Fisher.' Was Bett Beuley the same person as Bet Flint?

5. The author of the *Juvenile Adventures* (London, 1759) suggests that Kitty was riding from about the age of 14. It is Horace Bleackley, in *Ladies Fair and Frail* (London, 1906), who asserts that it was Dick Berenger who taught Kitty to ride. Bleackley dates the commencement of Kitty's riding lessons to around 1757, when Kitty was 16.

6. Richard Berenger was born 27 November 1719 and christened 17 December 1719 at St Martin in the Fields, the eldest of the three sons of Moses and Penelope Berenger. Penelope was the youngest daughter of Sir Richard Temple MP, 3rd Baronet. Her brother, Richard, became 1st Viscount Cobham. In 1771, a second book by Berenger was published, *The History and Art of Horsemanship*. Berenger served as George III's Gentleman of the Horse until his death in 1782 when the position was abolished.

7. *Thraliana: The Diary of Mrs Hester Lynch Thrale (later Mrs Piozzi), 1776–1809*; vol. 1 (1776–1784) (Clarendon Press, 1942). *London Chronicle*, 31 July 1759.

8. The ball at Dublin Castle was held in October 1748. Horace Walpole writing to Horace Mann, 18 June 1751.

9. After his uncle died in 1763, Thomas Hutchings adopted his surname, becoming Thomas Hutchings Medlycott. The 'Histories of the Tête-à-Tête annex'd: or, Memoirs of the Universal Gallant and the Cyprian Votary' in the *Town and Country Magazine or Universal Repository of Knowledge, Instruction, and Entertainment* for October 1779 makes a further claim about Thomas Hutchings Medlycott. The article says that the actress Peg Woffington was infatuated with Hutchings. Her anguish at his preference for Kitty, claimed the

magazine, contributed to her early death. Peg Woffington was taken ill on stage on 3 May 1757, with a paralysis. She was an invalid until her death on 28 March 1760. As Kitty was still with Anthony Martin at the date of Peg's collapse on stage, it seems unlikely that this claim is true. However, the information in the Tête-à-Tête echoes the account of Don Allenzo in the *Juvenile Adventures* closely enough to provide confirmation of Hutching's and Kitty's short-lived amour. *The Court of Cupid* (London, 1770) by Edward Thompson.

10. Joseph Mawbey was born on 2 December 1730. Later an MP, he was often a figure of ridicule, not least for his practice of keeping pigs. He was lampooned as 'Sir Joseph Hogstie' in the *Town and Country Magazine; or, Universal Repository of Knowledge, Instruction, and Entertainment for October 1780* in the article, 'Histories of the Tête-à-Tête annexed: or, Memoirs of Sir J. Hogstie, and Mrs Fl_yd.' This recounted his love life including his play for Kitty and her disinterest. He married in 1760 (to Elizabeth Pratt, his first cousin once removed), and in 1765, was created a baronet.

11. *The Juvenile Adventures of Miss Kitty Fisher* (London, 1759). William Whately called Robert Carey Sumner 'the best schoolmaster...' in a letter to John Grimston, 24 September 1771 (*History of Harrow School, 1324–1991*, Christopher Tyerman, Oxford University Press, 2000). William Brightwell Sumner returned to England in 1770 after a disagreement with Robert Clive (otherwise known as Clive of India) and bought Hatchlands Park near Guildford in Surrey.

12. In *The Juvenile Adventures of Miss Kitty Fisher* (London, 1759), it was claimed that Jane's mother sold her daughter's virginity to their landlord to cover the rent that she was otherwise unable to pay. The landlord sent the bailiffs in despite this and Jane's mother ended up in a debtor's prison, where she died. This is entirely false. Jane's mother was Hannah Sumner and her will reveals her to be a widow living at Eton in 1746. Far from being a debtor, Hannah owned three houses and had paid the mortgages of these off while a widow. She also left money to her three children and a quantity of silverware, gold watches, etc. Hannah Sumner was buried on 6 November 1746 at New Windsor, Berkshire. Jane was probably around 11 years of age at her mother's death and was left to the care of her paternal uncle, Dr John Sumner, Eton's headmaster. NA PROB 11/752/91: Will of Hannah Sumner of Eton, Buckinghamshire, 9 January 1747.

13. In the 1770s, Lady Caroline Fitzroy was barred from 'The Female Coterie' (a group of aristocratic ladies who met socially, the female equivalent of the gentlemen's clubs so prevalent in the capital). In retaliation, she set up a rival group, 'The New Female Coterie'. They met in a brothel and counted several 'fallen women' amongst their members. Robert Ashe (www.ashefamily.info/wp-content/uploads/2011/10/Miss-Elizabeth-Ashe1.pdf) makes a plausible argument for Elizabeth Ashe's father being William Windham (sometimes referred to as William Windham Ashe), MP for Aldeburgh and Helston. Edward Wortley Montagu's first marriage took place at the Fleet on 10 January 1730. His second, to Elizabeth Ashe, was performed at the May Fair Chapel,

21 July 1751. Elizabeth later married Robert Faulknor, RN. It was Horace Walpole, who knew her well, who nicknamed her 'the Pollard Ashe'. The claim that Kitty modelled herself on Elizabeth Chudleigh, Lady Harrington and Elizabeth Ashe is to be found in *Histoire de la Vie et des Aventures de la Duchesse de Kingston* (London, 1789). There were rumours that the Earl of Harrington later paid court to Kitty, who rebuffed him.

14. The letter was dated 28 January 1758. However, it is harking back to the 'old-style' year which, until 1752, began on 25 March, and was clearly written in 1759 from other subjects discussed (Garrick's performance of *Antony and Cleopatra* and General Wolfe commanding the expedition to Quebec) and lends credence to the idea that Kitty and Anthony Martin had parted in the latter months of 1758, forcing Kitty to launch herself onto the town in a bid to retain the lifestyle she had come to enjoy. *Ninth Report of the Royal Commission on Historical Manuscripts, Part II* (H. M. Stationery Office, 1884).

Chapter 3

1. *Correspondence of Emily, Duchess of Leinster (1731–1814), volume III, Letters of Lady Louisa Conolly and William, Marquis of Kildare (2nd Duke of Leinster)*, edited by Brian Fitzgerald. Emily FitzGerald was known as the Countess of Kildare between 1747 and 1761, the Marchioness of Kildare until 1766, and the Duchess of Leinster.

2. Lord Waldegrave and Maria Walpole married, by special licence and at her father's house, on 15 May 1759. Catherine, Lady Walpole was estranged from her husband, Robert Walpole, who lived openly with his mistress, Maria Skerrett, the daughter of a wealthy Irish merchant. After his wife's death, Walpole married Maria Skerrett but their union was short-lived as she died following a miscarriage. The Duke of Gloucester's marital transgression came to light when a second brother, Prince Henry, Duke of Cumberland and Strathearn, also – in the eyes of the royal family – married 'beneath him'. Prince Henry's bride was Anne Horton, the daughter of an Irish baron (Simon Luttrell, later the 1st Earl of Carhampton) and widow of Christopher Horton, a commoner, albeit a wealthy one. The king's anger at Prince Henry and Anne Horton's marriage led to the passing of the 1772 Royal Marriages Act which forbade any descendant of George II from marrying without the sovereign's consent. The king was therefore incandescent with rage when he discovered Prince William Henry, Duke of Gloucester had also taken a wife who didn't meet his approval, and which the new act had no bearing on. He banned Maria, Duchess of Gloucester, from appearing at court.

3. *The Juvenile Adventures of Miss Kitty Fisher* (London, 1759).

4. The 2nd Earl Poulett was a twin, born first ahead of his brother, the Hon. Peregrine Poulett. Many of Kitty's contemporaries adopted a surname. Kitty's anglicised surname of Fisher was the one that captured the imagination of the public, however. Sir Charles Bingham's wife had a fortune of £20,000. *The Juvenile Adventures of Miss Kitty Fisher*, vol. 2 (London, 1759).

5. Edmund Pyle writing to Samuel Kerrich, 11 January 1755. The 1st Baron Montfort consulted various surgeons as to the 'best' way of shooting oneself in the head. He had lost a fortune playing Hazard at White's, where he spent the last night of his life, staying until one o'clock in the morning before going home 'in a strange mood'. The ruinous estate inherited in 1755 by the 2nd Baron Montfort was eventually sold to pay off his debts. *Light Come, Light Go: Gambling, Gamester, Wagers, The Turf* by Ralph Nevill. British Library, Add. MS 32864, f. 524: Montfort to Newcastle, 11 May 1765; Appendix 4: List of Sitting Members of the House of Lords (1760–1811) who Received Pensions or Annuities to Support their Rank. Parliamentary History, 28.

6. Thomas Bromley, 2nd Baron Montfort did not marry until 1772; his bride was Mary Anne, daughter of Andrew Blake of St Kitts and Montserrat and the sister of Sir Patrick Blake, 1st Baronet. William Cole wrote to Horace Walpole on 16 September 1771, noting with acidity that 'Lord Montfort is going to be married to Miss Blake, sister to Mr Blake who married Sir Charles Bunbury's sister. Most people think the lady has good courage.' *The Yale Edition of Horace Walpole's Correspondence*, edited by W. S. Lewis, vol. 1 (via Yale University Digital Collections).

7. *Westminster Magazine*, 1773. Jane's daughter, Louisa, was christened at St George, Hanover Square on 5 July 1760. In the baptism register, her parents are named Jane and William Missington, although the latter is probably really William Skrine, whom Jane married in 1764. Shortly after Louisa's birth, John Montagu, 4th Earl of Sandwich fell in love with the 17-year-old singer, Martha Ray. They lived as a married couple, having several children together until, in 1779, Martha was murdered outside the Covent Garden theatre by James Hackman. 'Histories of the Tête-à-Tête annexed: or, Memoirs of Lord M___t and Mrs L__b__d' in *The Town and Country Magazine, or, Universal Repository of Knowledge, Instruction, and Entertainment* for February, 1780.

8. *The Town and Country Magazine; or, Universal Repository of Knowledge, Instruction, and Entertainment* for February 1780: 'Histories of the Tête-à-Tête annexed: or, Memoirs of Lord M__t and Mrs L__b__d.'

9. For more detail on faro, and Georgian gambling in general, see *The Georgian Art of Gambling* by Claire Cock-Starkey.

10. *The Juvenile Adventures of Miss Kitty Fisher* (London, 1759)

11. The fifth man was referred to in *The Juvenile Adventures of Miss Kitty Fisher* (London, 1759) as the Chevalier de Cumaro but other than allowing Kitty the share of his winnings he did not incline to allow her anything more. 'Our life here would not displease you, for we eat and drink well, and the Earl [of Coventry] holds a faro-bank every night to us, which we have plundered considerably' (Gilly Williams to George Selwyn, 1752). On 30 July 1752, George James (Gilly) Williams married Diana Coventry, the Earl of Coventry's sister. *Blackwood's Edinburgh Magazine*, vol. 15, January–June 1844.

12. *A Venetian Affair* (Knopf, 2003), Andrea di Robilant. Giustiniana Wynne was resident in London for several months during 1760. Kitty's spat with

the Countess of Coventry was recounted in *The Juvenile Adventures of Miss Kitty Fisher* (London, 1759) so the incident was talked about for some time afterwards.

13. The story of Kitty having a cold and the peers and MPs being denied admittance is recounted in *Histoire de la Vie et des Aventures de la Duchesse de Kingston* (London, 1789).

Chapter 4

1. *London Evening Post*, 12–14 May 1757, *London Chronicle*, 13–15 March 1759 and *Lloyd's Evening Post*, 14–16 March 1759. The letter giving this information was signed D. B. in the last, but as D. Burgess in the *London Chronicle*.

2. Further clues that Samuel Derrick was the author of the *Juvenile Adventures of Miss Kitty Fisher* (London, 1759) are to be found in the *Town and Country Magazine* for April 1769. After Derrick's death, they devoted four pages to anecdotes of his life. In it, is the claim that, as a writer he was 'of great service to the fair … he wrote panegyrics upon their charms, introduced them to his friends, and apologized to their creditors. Among the number of these ladies who were the most distinguished, was Santa Charlotta, Miss B_ll, L[uc]y C[oope]r, the famous Miss Kitty F[ishe]r, and even the now pompous and celebrated Mrs. L[essingha]m.' Samuel Derrick was the anonymous author of *Memoirs of the Bedford Coffee-House* (the author was just named 'a genius'). In that, Derrick relates a dispute that took place in the Bedford over the actress Maria Isabella Nossiter. This lady is mentioned in the *Juvenile Adventures*, in the chapter which Derrick has written himself into. Kitty is supposed to be auditioning for John Rich, who asks, 'do you mouth well? Miss Nossero [Nossiter] has brought it entirely into vogue from the tall Irishman [Maria Nossiter's lover, the actor Spranger Barry]'. In the 2nd volume of the *Memoirs of the Bedford Coffee-House*, a series of letters are added at the end. One, signed Fulminator, asserts that 'it was me that debauched L[uc]y C[oope]r, and introduced K[itt]y F[ishe]r upon the town.' *The Meretriciad* (1761) described Jane as 'witty Sumner'. In *The Juvenile Adventures*, Kitty's mother is referred to as Kate, which is an oddity when all the other information regarding Kitty's family is correct. Perhaps, if Kitty was involved in the writing of this pseudo-memoir, naming her mother was one step too far? *The Juvenile Adventures* was also issued in a truncated version as *The Uncommon Adventures of Miss Kitty F****r* (London, 1759).

3. Joseph Salvador (aka Joseph Jessurun Rodrigues) was born in 1716 into an English Shepardi family from Holland.

4. *Public Advertiser*, 27 March 1759.

5. Kent Archives and Local History Centre, U771: Deeds of the Osborne Family (1282–1924): U771/C7/115, Letter from George Woodward, vicar of East Hendred, Berkshire to his uncle, George London at Long Kitton near Kingston, Surrey, dated 6 April 1759. Woodward's story about Kitty at the theatre was in reply to his uncle's previous letter; her infamy was already such

that she was being discussed in private letters between a country vicar and his uncle. The Duke of Grafton was Woodward's patron. *Histoire de la Vie et des Aventures de la Duchesse de Kingston* (London, 1789). *Elizabeth: The Scandalous Life of an 18th Century Duchess* by Claire Gervat (Random House, 2011).

6. A. P. Baggs and R. J. E. Bush, 'Parishes: Hinton St. George', in *A History of the County of Somerset: Volume 4*, ed. R W Dunning (London, 1978), via British History Online. During the early 1700s, Lord Poulett's father had made alterations to the park surrounding the house, and these were continued by the 2nd earl's younger brother, Vere Poulett, 3rd Earl Poulett. The Norwich born architect, Matthew Brettingham's account book, 1747–64, records payments for works undertaken at Hinton St George.

7. George Grenville, the younger brother of Richard Grenville-Temple, 2nd Earl Temple, later became the Prime Minister of Great Britain (1763–1765). Letter dated 17 April 1759, included in *The Grenville Papers*, vol. I (London, 1852). Although Jenkinson claimed that Kitty had gone down into Devonshire with Lord Poulett. It is more likely that they had gone to Poulett's estate, Hinton St George, which is less than 10 miles from the Devonshire/Somerset county border. Elizabeth Montagu's letter to Mrs Carter quoted in *Elizabeth Montagu, the Queen of the Blue-Stockings: Her Correspondence from 1720 to 1761 by her great-great-niece Emily J. Climenson*, vol. II (John Murray, London, 1906). Mrs Montagu said that 'Miss Kitty Fisher modestly asked Earl Pembroke to make her a Countess.' The letter was written in April 1759 just when it was rumoured Kitty and Earl Poulett would marry. Henry Herbert, 10th Earl of Pembroke was already married; three years earlier Lady Elizabeth Spencer, daughter of the 3rd Duke of Marlborough, had become his wife.

8. Keppel's mother, Lady Anne Lennox, was the daughter of the 1st Duke of Richmond; his father was Willem van Keppel, 2nd Earl of Albermarle and a personal friend of King George II. Unfortunately for Augustus, his father frittered away the family's fortune. Reynolds painted Keppel's portrait during 1759 as well as Kitty's, and so Keppel must have sat for the artist early in the year. In November 1759, during the battle of Quiberon Bay on stormy seas off the French coast, Keppel showed mercy and common decency when he sent out boats to rescue the crew of a French ship of the line. Under Keppel's command, his ship, the *Torbay*, had been firing upon the *Thésée*. Both ships were evenly matched, having seventy-four guns each, but the Thésée made a sudden change of course and water poured through her open ports. As she foundered before his eyes, Keppel ordered boats to be launched to save as many of the French crew as was humanly possible. His action saved around twenty French sailors from the wreck of the *Thésée*, the rest perished. The Battle of Quiberon Bay took place during the Seven Years' War.

9. Lady Burlington's portrait by Joshua Reynolds was a full-length, painted in 1780 when she was Lady Elizabeth Compton. Two years later, she married George Cavendish, 1st Earl of Burlington. It was while sitting for a portrait by Sir Francis Grant that Lady Burlington recounted her experience of being

painted by Reynolds, and the anecdote was relayed by William Powell Frith, R. A., in volume II of *My Autobiography and Reminiscences* (Harper & Brothers, New York, 1888).

10. Nicholas Penny, writing in *Reynolds: Catalogue of a Royal Academy of Arts Exhibition* (1986) puts forth the theory that Reynolds perhaps stood to gain from prints of his portraits, saying that 'we do not know what professional advantage, or exactly what share, if any, in the profits was involved for Reynolds in such cases, but we suppose that the initiative was probably his.' *The Juvenile Adventures of Miss Kitty Fisher* (London, 1759).

11. The dates of Kitty's appointments with Reynolds comes from his pocketbook. In 1759, during these three months, she sat for the painter on 18, 21, 24 and 26 April, 1, 4, 8, 9, 10, 17, 21, 22, 27, and 30 May, 8, and 24 June (with a cancellation on 7 May). Dates are given in *Reynolds: Catalogue of a Royal Academy of Arts Exhibition* (1986). *Middlesex Journal*, 14–17 October 1769. The letter from Fresnoy contains inaccuracies as it relates to Kitty, however, believing her still alive and calling her a tailor's maid. www.pastellists.com/Articles/WILLS.pdf. *Joshua Reynolds: The Life and Times of the First President of the Royal Academy* by Ian McIntyre.

12. The portrait is now held at Petworth House in Sussex. It was acquired, before 1835, by George O'Brien Wyndham, 3rd Earl of Egremont, a noted art collector, and it descended in his family to the 3rd Lord Leconfield who, at his death in 1952, gave Petworth and its contents to the nation. Nicholas Penny, in *Reynolds: Catalogue of a Royal Academy of Arts Exhibition* (1986) quotes Northcote.

13. *A Venetian Affair*, Andrea di Robilant (Knopf, 2003). *Public Advertiser*, 19 and 20 June 1759, *Histoire de la Vie et des Aventures de la Duchesse de Kingston* (London, 1789). *The Letters of Horace Walpole, Earl of Orford*, volume 9 (R. Bentley, 1859).

14. *Public Advertiser*, 12 and 18 May 1759.

15. Pliny the Elder told the story of Cleopatra and the pearl. Hogarth's portrait of Sigismunda didn't sell in his lifetime. It passed to his wife, and then to her cousin before it was bought in a sale at Greenwood's in 1790; in 1879 it was bequeathed to the Tate Gallery. It is not known if Reynolds had seen Hogarth's portrait; if he had, it would have been at a private viewing. In *William Hogarth's Sigismunda in focus* (London, Tate Britain, 2000), Marcia Pointon says that Reynolds's Cleopatra was 'quite possibly as an artistic snub to Hogarth (demonstrating how an Italianate heroine might properly be conveyed)'. The remaining dates for Kitty's appointments with Reynolds are 22 August, 20 October, 29 November and 4, 10, and 12 December: dates given in *Reynolds: Catalogue of a Royal Academy of Arts Exhibition* (1986). *Kenwood, Paintings in the Iveagh Bequest* by Julie Bryant (Yale University Press, 2003). The portrait of Lady Betty Felton as Cleopatra is held at Kingston Lacy in Dorset, a National Trust property. In 1848, Beriah Botfield, Esq., of Norton Hall, Northamptonshire, owned a miniature copy by William Booth of Sir Joshua Reynolds's portrait of Kitty Fisher as *Cleopatra Dissolving the Pearl*. It

was said to have been copied from the original and was 8½" x 7½". Like the supposed Hogarth of Kitty owed by Botfield, this miniature was most likely left, in Botfield's will, to the Marquess of Bath. It may be contemporaneous with the one which, in 1903, was in the 3rd Baron Hylton's collection of miniatures at Ammerdown House. It claimed to depict Kitty Fisher. No artist was named. The portrait was half-length and Kitty was described as seated, wearing a white dress with blue bows. *Catalogue of Pictures in the Collection of Beriah Botfield, Esq. at Norton Hall* (London, 1848), *Catalogue of Pictures, Drawings and Miniatures, the Property of Lord Hylton* (privately printed, 1903).

16. Sir Charles Bingham paid Reynolds 10 guineas before 1 December 1760 (as per a record in Reynolds's ledger) but didn't pay any more until 1774. However, he seems not to have taken possession of the portrait. With his fortune in need of a boost, Bingham had married in the summer of 1760. His wife, Margaret, daughter of Sir James Smith of Bath, was herself a talented artist. Even though she might have appreciated Kitty's portrait as a work of art, it would be a stretch to have her husband's ex-lover exhibited in her home. Via his daughter, Lavinia, who married George Spencer, 2nd Earl Spencer, Charles Bingham is the ancestor of Diana, Princess of Wales. In 1776, Reynolds's ledger records a payment of 35 guineas from 'Mr Parker for Sir Charles' picture, sent to Saltram'. The advertisement for the prints and detail on the inscription written underneath, *London Chronicle*, 12–14 July and 8–11 September 1759. The 'Cleopatra' portrait was sold at Christie's on 10 June 1876 for 2,350 guineas. It was exhibited in Yorkshire by Mr J Beckett in June 1881. It came into the collection of Edward Guinness, 1st Earl Iveagh of Kenwood who left Kenwood and its contents to the nation at his death, in the Iveagh Bequest. A copy of this portrait ended up in India, probably taken there by the man for whom it was painted, the Danish governor of Serampore, Colonel Ole Bie. He died in 1805 and the picture was brought to England by Bie's friend, Joshua Marsham. Dr Busteed saw it in Marsham's widow's house in 1887, and that lady bequeathed it to her daughter, Mrs Rowe. However, the family believed the sitter in the portrait to be Mme Grand, and that it was painted by Johan Zoffany. While it was Kitty in the portrait, it is unclear if the artist was Reynolds or whether this was a copy by another hand. *Bengal Past and Present*, vol XXXVII, Part 1, serial no. 73, January – March 1929 and *The Times*, 12 July 1929.

17. *London Chronicle*, 31 July 1759.

18. *Kitty Fisher's Merry Thought; or No Joke like a True Joke* was advertised in *The Public Ledger*, 8 March 1760 and *The Public Advertiser*, 21 February 1761. In the latter, it was listed as being for sale for 2s from the same printer who had just published the 1761 *Harris's List*. There is no full-length portrait of Kitty known to exist, but one of Fanny Murray dating from 1754 in which she is holding a sheet of music was relabelled and reissued around this time with Kitty's name attached. The Victoria and Albert Museum holds copies of both prints under reference numbers S.2919-2009 and S.1161-2009. Paul Sandby may have drawn Kitty Fisher. The Royal Collection Trust holds a watercolour

by Sandby (RCIN 914376) of a woman dressed as a milkmaid which is inscribed with her name on the reverse. The British Museum holds a different sketch by Sandby on which, again, Kitty's name is written on the back (ref no. 1904,0819.572).

19. The story of Kitty and Prince Edward is given in *The Juvenile Adventures of Miss Kitty Fisher* (London, 1759) where Edward is called 'a Nobleman of the House of Castile'. However, the tale is given some credence by Horace Walpole, relating the conversation between the Prince of Wales and Prince Frederick concerning Kitty. Horace Walpole writing to Montagu, 16 May 1759, *Horace Walpole's Correspondence with George Montagu*, vol. 1, edited by W. S. Lewis and Ralph St. Brown, Jr. (Yale University Press, 1941). Prince Edward was created Duke of York and Albany almost a year after his encounter with Kitty, on 1 April 1760.

20. *The Town and Country Magazine, or, Universal Repository of Knowledge, Instruction, and Entertainment* for April 1770. The Tête-à-Tête article on Earl Ligonier within the *Town and Country Magazine* was titled 'Memoirs of the Old Soldier and Hebe W_ts_n'. The girl in question, Hebe Watson, had been a young servant in the earl's household, so the writer claimed. Ligonier was rewarded with his earldom upon his retirement from the post of commander-in-chief of the army (due to increasing ill-health) in 1766. His only known child was his daughter, Penelope, born 8 January 1727 and christened eleven days later at St Martin-in-the-Fields. Her mother was Penelope Miller of Southwark. Penelope Ligonier married Lt Col Arthur Graham in 1748. Both the kevenhuller and nivernois hats, in vogue in the early years of the century, were tricorns, but while the latter was small and neat, the former was much larger and heavier dragoon style with gold braid. *Hats: A History of Fashion in Headwear*, Hilda Amphlett (Courier Corporation, 2012).

21. *The European Magazine: And London Review*, volume 23, 1793. It seems likely that the review of the troops was either the one held in early May or in mid-July 1759 when Kitty was at the zenith of her fame. George II attended both. At the former he was there with his son, Prince Edward, Sir John Ligonier and 'a great number of persons of distinction'. William Pitt is not specifically mentioned as being there. Pitt was, however, certainly present at the latter, together with the king and the Prince of Wales, as he wrote about it in a letter to his wife (although he – perhaps wisely – does not mention meeting any ladies). *The British Chronicle*, 8–10 May 1759, *Public Advertiser*, 18 July 1759, *Whitehall Evening Post*, 14–17 July 1759, and *Correspondence of William Pitt, Earl of Chatham*, vol. II (John Murray, 1838).

22. *Whitehall Evening Post*, 24–26 April 1759.

Chapter 5

1. The anecdote concerning the harp is recounted in *Histoire de la Vie et des Aventures de la Duchesse de Kingston* (London, 1789). The Earl of Sandwich isn't mentioned by name, but the description appears to indicate he is the man referred to.

2. Perhaps Fanny, in her *Memoirs*, was obscuring her true parentage just enough to hide the identity of her family, or maybe she was disguising a possible Jewish ancestry, for there is a baptism dated 23 August 1728 at St Michael in the centre of Bath for Frances, daughter of Isaac Rudman.
3. *Correspondence of Emily, Duchess of Leinster (1731–1814)* (Dublin, 1957). Lady Northampton was Lady Ann Somerset, eldest daughter of the 4th Duke of Beaufort, who had married Charles Compton, 7th Earl of Northampton just over a month earlier, on 13 September 1759.
4. I am indebted to the research of Stephen Leach (Keele University) on the portrait, 'Two Girls Dressing a Kitten by Candlelight' by Joseph Wright of Derby (www.academia.edu/33348558/Miss_Kitty.docx). Quote on the use of cats in Dutch art from *Joseph Wright in Liverpool* by Elizabeth E. Barker (Yale University Press, 2007). Joseph Wright's painting is now located at Kenwood, along with the Cleopatra portrait of Kitty by Reynolds.
5. Following on from Kitty's appointments with Reynolds at the end of 1759 (20 October, 29 November and 4, 10, and 12 December), Kitty had one appointment early in 1760, on 2 February. She did not sit for Reynolds again until December 1760. The portrait was unsold during Reynolds's lifetime and, in a 1796 sale of his paintings, was bought by John Joshua Proby, 1st Earl of Carysfort (at Greenwood's, London) in a sale of Reynolds's effects, after his death. Lord Carysfort paid £4 18s for the painting. It is a half figure, nearly full face and measures 29½" x 23½". The earl was one of the pall-bearers at Reynolds's funeral. The painting still hangs at the earl's ancestral home, Elton Hall. Information on the painting via Elton Hall.
6. The letter was dated 17 October 1748.
7. Kitty is said to have a good grasp of the French language in 'Histories of the Tête-à-Tête annexed; or, Memoirs of the Old Soldier and Hebe W-ts-n', *The Town and Country Magazine: or, Universal Repository of Knowledge, Instruction, and Entertainment* for April 1770.
8. Casanova said that the man who lit Kitty's punch with the banknote was the 'Chevalier Stihens, Mr Pitt's brother-in-law'. *Memoirs de Jacques Casanova de Seingalt, écrits par lui-même* (1871). Fanny Murray remained a faithful wife to David Ross, the couple living together until Fanny died in 1778. For all that Casanova's memoirs ring false with regard to Kitty, in the same paragraph as he recalls Goudar introducing him to Kitty, there is also substantiated truth. Goudar introduced Casanova to 'a girl of sixteen, a veritable prodigy of beauty, who served at the bar of a tavern at which we took a bottle of strong beer. She was an Irishwoman and a Catholic and was named Sarah. I should have liked to get possession of her, but Goudar had views of his own on the subject and carried her off the next year. He ended by marrying her, and she was the Sara Goudar who shone at Naples, Florence, Venice, and elsewhere.' Possibly, Goudar and Sarah married at Kensington on 20 April 1765, if so, Goudar's forename (Pierre) was Anglicised to Peter, and Sarah's surname was Ker. The couple had left London by the early part of 1765. They travelled to Italy and

while in Naples, Sarah Goudar reputedly seduced Ferdinand, King of Naples and the Two Sicilies.

9. *Histoire de la Vie et des Aventures de la Duchesse de Kingston* (London, 1789). The account went on to say that 'some politicians grumbled about the excess, but the public liked Kitty for it.' Kitty may have published an account of it, which praised her lover.

10. *A Collection of Miscellaneous Essays* by Thomas Mozeen (London 1762).

11. *The Correspondence of Horace Walpole, with George Montagu, Esq., and Others: 1760–1769* (Henry Colburn, 1837). Earl Ferrers pleaded insanity but was found guilty and condemned to death. Despite being a peer of the realm, he was treated as a common criminal and hanged at Tyburn on 5 May 1760.

12. Horace Walpole to Horace Mann, 1 November 1760. Maria was, in fact, just 28 years of age.

13. Maria, Countess of Coventry's death was traditionally believed to be due to lead poisoning, although tuberculosis was also suggested. In the summer of 1759, Maria's apothecary was prescribing medicine which was used to treat tuberculosis. Her death would therefore appear to be very much a combination of the two. The author of *The Meretriciad* (1761) talked about Madame de Pompadour's use of skin-whitening make-up before mentioning Jane: 'With witty Sumner, have you lately been? Was it at tea? before she'd time to clean! Did you not stare to see her pebbl'd face? Observe it now! with ev'ry blooming grace.' *The Courtesan* by Edward Thompson (London, 1765).

Chapter 6

1. William Richard Chetwynd was born on 2 October 1731 at the family's London home, Portland House in Greek Street (now nos. 12–13), Soho. He was christened ten days later at St Anne's in Soho. He was the youngest child of his family. *Stamford Mercury*, 7 October 1731. His wife was the daughter of William Wollaston, MP. Elizabeth Chetwynd, William's daughter, was christened 14 May 1757 at St George's, Hanover Square and named for her mother (she was left a bequest by her grandmother, Elizabeth Wollaston, in her will dated 1763 (NA, PROB 11/900/171)). On 17 March 1774, at St Marylebone, this daughter married John Parson, Esq. of Parndon in Essex, the son of a wealthy West India merchant.

2. *London Evening Post*, 3–5 July 1759, the *Surrey Mirror*, 27 September 1884 and *The Antiquarian Magazine & Bibliographer*, Volume 3, 1883. The manor house that Kitty lived in was mostly demolished in the 1770s and a new house built in its place. Until Gresham began his remodelling of Titsey, he leased out the old building. It was in this way that Kitty and William Chetwynd became two of the last tenants of the old mansion house. Historic England website, www.historicengland.org.uk/lisiting/the-list/list-entry/1000121. One small wing from the manor house in which Kitty lived has survived, attached to the present mansion, and used historically as servants' quarters.

3. *St James's Chronicle or the British Evening Post*, 21–23 July 1761. Barbara St John and Lord Coventry married on 27 September 1764.

4. Polly Davis was born c.1742/3. In 1764, Joshua Reynolds painted the first of several portraits of her and, as he had with Kitty, established Polly as a person of note. Polly later married Alexander Nesbitt, a merchant banker, and then became the mistress of the Hon Augustus John Hervey (who had secretly married Elizabeth Chudleigh). *The Diaries of a Duchess. Extracts from the Diaries of the First Duchess of Northumberland (1716–1776)* (Hodder & Stoughton, 1926).

5. It remains unknown how Mary Banks acquired her additional surname but Charles Powlett, 5th Duke of Bolton's servants knew her as Mrs Brown, the duke's housekeeper. She bore the duke a short-lived son and a daughter, Jean Mary Banks Brown, who went on to inherit her father's estate. Jean Mary's husband, Thomas Orde, added his wife's surname onto his own, becoming Thomas Orde-Powlett. The couple were later created Baron and Baroness Bolton, to make up for the loss of the dukedom. For more on the 5th Duke of Bolton and Mary Banks, see *A History of the Dukes of Bolton, 1600–1815: Love Loyalty* by Joanne Major and Sarah Murden (Pen & Sword Books, 2020).

6. In *The Meretriciad* (1761), Thompson puts a notation against the name Mrs Brown, stating it to be Kitty's 'name as house-keeper'.

7. *The Town and Country Magazine, or, Universal Repository of Knowledge, Instruction, and Entertainment* for March 1769. A Valentine Haughton (age unknown) was buried at Hanover, Jamaica, on 27 May 1756. In the Jamaican baptism register, there are two entries for children of a Valentine and Ann Haughton, Mary (christened 29 October 1749 at Westmoreland and Richard, christened 24 February 1752 at Hanover). With no further proof, it is impossible to know whether these two infants were Nancy Parsons's children, nor whether Valentine was her pseudo-husband. All that can be said is that there was a mercantile family named Haughton living at Hanover on the island of Jamaica, and Nancy's lover would appear to be one of them. The story is recalled a little differently in the Grenville Papers which recounts that Nancy 'became weary of a residence in the West Indies: she escaped from her lover by stratagem' and returned to London.

8. C. Cooper, perfumier, advertised his 'Naples Dew, or Italian Drop' which was 'beautifying and preserving' for ladies' and gentlemen's skin in the *Public Advertiser*, 7 March 1765; he even claimed that washing the eyes with a few drops mixed with water would strengthen the vision. The Science Museum in London holds an earthenware dispensing pot upon which is written, 'Cooper, Perfumer, Brewer Street'. Caroline, Countess of Harrington, was the 3rd Duke of Grafton's aunt.

9. Information on Kitty's letter printed in the 1761 edition of *Harris's List* taken from *The Covent Garden Ladies* (Tempus, 2006) by Hallie Rubenhold.

10. The historian of *Harris's List*, Hallie Rubenhold, describes Kitty's inclusion as a 'semi-absent presence'. For more information on the 1761 edition of the list,

and Kitty's letter, see *Harris's List of Covent Garden Ladies: Sex in the City in Georgian Britain* (Tempus, 2005) *and The Covent Garden Ladies: Pimp General Jack and the Extraordinary Story of Harris's List* (Tempus, 2005), both by Hallie Rubenhold. *A Sketch of the Present Times, and the Times to Come in an Address to Kitty Fisher* (London, 1762).

11. Leslie and Taylor, in volume 1 of *Life and Times of Sir Joshua Reynolds* (J. Murray, 1865), list eight sittings for 'a' Miss Fisher during August 1761, noting that they were generally on days when no one else came after her. There is an additional note in Reynolds's pocketbook that one of Miss Fisher's portraits was to be sent to M. Breitenhagh, the Secretary of the Dutch Embassy in Scotland Yard, 'when the print is finished'. This may be for one of the 'doves' portraits. However, in *Reynolds*, edited by Nicholas Penny (Royal Academy of Arts, 1986), it is asserted that Kitty did not sit at all to Joshua Reynolds in 1761. Kitty's appointments with Reynolds in the first two months of 1762 were 8, 14, 19, and 21 January and 2 February. There are three known versions of Joshua Reynolds's portrait of Kitty with a pair of doves, each with subtle differences. The first of the three to be painted was possibly the one which is now held by the New York Public Library. It was engraved in 1762, so must have been painted 1761/2. The locket around her name is said to show David Garrick, but it seems unlikely that he would be depicted as he has little importance in Kitty's life. At the time, Kitty was with William Richard Chetwynd, so one would expect his image to be in the locket if he had commissioned the portrait. However, as no such detail has survived, it must also be a probability that the person the painting was first intended for asked for his image to be shown. The original owner of this portrait is unknown. By the mid-1800s it was in the possession of Colonel James Lenox of New York. When he sold it in 1845, the catalogue said that it was painted for the family from whom it had been obtained by an art dealer and sold on via Colnaghi & Co. to Lenox. The colonel bequeathed the painting to the New York Public Library. The second version of the Doves portrait was sold for £210 in 1830, and ended up in the Novar Collection amassed by Hugh Andrew Johnstone Munro, of Novar. He was the artist Joseph Mallord William Turner's friend and executor. The Novar Collection was sold in 1878. Kitty's portrait fetched 700 guineas, a lot less than some of the Turners in the sale. The small miniature of the man in the locket worn around Kitty's neck is different from the one held in the NYPL. His nose appears more bulbous. In 1889, this portrait was sold again (for £105) and then it fetched 1,300 guineas in Christie's 1895 sale of the Hodgson Collection. The last of the three paintings of Kitty with the doves is thought to have been completed at a later date, due to Kitty's hairstyle, which is in a style fashionable a decade or so after her death. It was sold to Lord Crewe by Reynolds as a portrait of Kitty Fisher. Lord Crewe made a first payment of 10 guineas before 1 December 1760 and a second payment of £52 10s in April 1774 for this painting. In contrast with the two earlier portraits, in this one, Kitty is not wearing a locket. The portrait hung at Crewe Hall and luckily

survived the 1866 fire that devastated the property. It was still there in 1871, in the large, gold drawing-room beside several other Reynolds portraits and a backgammon board which once belonged to Elizabeth I. By 1903, it was owned by Sir Charles Tennant, Baronet, and after his death by his son, Baron Glenconner. He installed a gallery in his house and allowed people to view his portraits. This portrait of Kitty was one of those on view. It is now in a private collection.

12. Mystery surrounds the Belvoir Castle portrait of Kitty by Reynolds. The Duke of Rutland bought it from Reynolds in 1782, for £52 10s, as a portrait of 'Miss Fisher', and it is listed in other records as depicting Kitty Fisher. No other details of it have survived. Max Michaelis, of Montebello, South Africa, owned a portrait of Kitty Fisher wearing a silver/blue dress and holding a fan. It had possibly been bought from the London dealers Dowdeswell & Dowdeswell before 1896 when it was valued in an insurance document for Michaelis. It remained in the family's private collection and was loaned for a time to the National Gallery of Art in Cape Town. Cecil Michaelis sold the portrait at Sotheby's (9 March 1988) to fund the construction of a design centre in the outbuildings at Montebello. *Old Masters and Aspirations: The Randlords, Art and South Africa* by Michael Stevenson, Thesis presented for the Degree of Doctor of Philosophy in the Department of Art History, University of Cape Town, September 1997. A photograph of this portrait can be found in *Reynolds*, edited by Nicholas Penny (Royal Academy of Arts, catalogue published in association with Weidenfeld and Nicolson, London, 1986). Included in the 1821 Thomond sale was a Reynolds portrait titled, *Lady with a parrot, head unfinished*. It was probably painted c.1763/64. After Reynolds's death, this painting remained in the possession of his niece, the Marchioness of Thomond. The buyer in 1821 was Thomas Phillips, R. A. After his death, it was sold by Christie's in 1846 for £220 10s to Farrer on behalf of Henry, 3rd Marquess Lansdowne. In 2007, this painting was sold at Sotheby's as a portrait of Kitty Fisher. It is now in a private collection.

13. Nelly O'Brien's third son by Sackville Tufton was another boy, Stanley, born 18 January 1768 (Alfred had been born 23 November 1764 and Sackville on 4 December 1765). All three boys were baptised at St George's in Hanover Square, and Nelly was buried in that same church on 2 April 1768, soon after the birth of her third son. For further information on Nelly and her sons, see www.georgianera.wordpress.com/2018/12/04/revealing-new-information-about-the-courtesan-nelly-obrien.

14. The tax records show the Carrington Street property in John Henry Fischer's name in 1762 and in Kitty's name (as Mrs Martin) the year after.

15. *Nollekens and His Times: Comprehending a Life of that Celebrated Sculptor: and Memoirs of Several Contemporary Artists, from the Time of Roubiliac, Hogarth and Reynolds to that of Fuseli, Flaxman and Blake*, Volume 1 by John Thomas Smith (Henry Colburn, 1828). Historical Portraits Image Library (www.historicalportraits.com). A watercolour miniature on ivory by Luke Sullivan

was sold at Sotheby's in 1975 as a Portrait of a Lady, possibly Kitty Fisher. It is dated 1763 (signed LS/1763). Dr Charles and Nathaniel Chauncy are the first known owners of this miniature; they sold it at Greenwood's in London in 1790 along with another miniature of Kitty by Rupert Barber. The buyer was Nathaniel Smith, who paid £1 3s for the Sullivan and Barber miniatures as one lot. When this miniature appeared again at Sotheby's, in 2008, the original frame had been replaced. Philip Mould, in his Historical Portraits Image Library, says that, following research in the catalogue of the 1975 sale, the border had been inscribed, 'leading to the credible identification of the sitter as Kitty Fisher'. He goes on to say that 'Sullivan probably became personally acquainted with Kitty Fisher through Reynolds and this portrait of her would appear to be partially based on an erotic sketch of her as Danaë executed by Reynolds [Berlin, Gemäldegalerie]. In this sketch a small dog, possibly the same dog she is seen holding here, is perched at the end of her couch.' Historical Portraits Image Library: www.historicalportraits.com/Gallery.asp?Page=Item&ItemID=150 4&Desc=Catherine-Maria-(Kitty)-Fisher-|-Luke-Sullivan; Sotheby's: www. sothebys.com/en/auctions/ecatalogue/2008/important-miniatures-from-a-private-collection-l08172/lot.11.html.

16. In 1829, in the sale of the belongings of Captain Marryat, C. B., of Sussex Villa in Fulham at Harry Phillips auction rooms in London, there was a portrait said to be of Kitty Fisher by William Hogarth. Three years later, at Edward Foster's auction rooms, a small whole length portrait of Kitty by Hogarth was sold for £10. It might be the same one included in a sale by a 'gentleman of distinguished taste and knowledge in the arts' just a few weeks later. In 1848, a portrait of Kitty Fisher by Hogarth was listed in the collection of Beriah Botfield of Norton Hall near Daventry, Northamptonshire. The only information given was its size: 4'1" x 3'4". After Botfield's death (in 1863), it was most likely included in the bequest he made to the Marquess of Bath, to whom he claimed to be distantly related. Then, in February 1881 at Messrs Morrison, Dick & McCulloch, a Hogarth of Kitty sold for 115 guineas. Possibly it was bought by the Earl of Egremont whose executors listed a portrait said to be Kitty and by Hogarth in May 1892, at Christie's. Finally, we have a description given. Kitty, in a red silk dress with lace sleeves, is shown playing the guitar. It sold for 190 guineas. It is unknown if this is the same portrait of Kitty Fisher by Hogarth in which she was described as 'seated, talking' that was sold by Christie's in 1896. Four years later, in New York, the sale of pictures from the collection of Albert D'Huyvetter of Antwerp included a portrait of Kitty Fisher by Hogarth. The portrait said to be of Kitty by Hogarth which hangs at Titsey Place is now thought to be by Philip Mercier and be of an earlier date. Getty Provenance Index, *Catalogue of Pictures in the Collection of Beriah Botfield, Esq. at Norton Hall* (London, 1848), Glasgow Herald, 5 February 1881, *Morning Post*, 23 May 1892, *Catalogue of an Important Sale of Original First Class Oil Paintings being the Entire Collection of Mr. A. D'Huyvetter of Antwerp to be sold at the Leeds Art Galleries, Nos. 817 and 819 Broadway* (New York, 1900). In June 1840

at Christie's, Joseph Marshland, Esq, sold a Thomas Gainsborough portrait in which the sitter was supposedly Kitty Fisher. It fetched £32 11s and was probably bought by Reece Bevan of Freckleton House in Wigan. In 1860, the painting was exhibited at the Wigan Mechanic's Institution and Bazaar where it was described as well-painted, with the neck and breast being especially fine. Reece Bevan's collection of paintings was sold in 1876, again by Christie's, and this portrait was included in that sale. The auction notes say that Kitty's 'pretty face' was 'nearly in profile' and that she wore 'a mob cap, white muslin chemisette, and brown muslin dress'. The portrait was bust size in a painted oval and 'more solid, not to say heavy, in the painting than Gainsborough usually is'. It fetched 95 guineas. As a comparison, a portrait of Georgiana, Duchess of Devonshire by Thomas Gainsborough in the same sale realised 10,100 guineas. In August 1883, the portrait of Kitty Fisher by Thomas Gainsborough was included in the Strawberry Hill sale. Its value had dropped even further as it was bought by the art dealer, Asher Wertheimer, for 80 guineas. The portrait included in the Saltaire Exhibition in 1887 was probably this one. A painting titled *Portrait of a Lady (Kitty Fisher)* by Gainsborough was included in the sale of the 'late Mr Holland Burne's effects at Bath'. It appears that the sitter's identity was being questioned at this point. It was said to come from the Shockerwick collection and the dimensions were given as 25" x 30". The portrait was sold in December 1911 and fetched £60. *Wigan Observer & District Advertiser*, 21 January 1860, *Manchester Courier & Lancashire General Advertiser*, 12 July 1869, *The Times*, 5 and 8 May 1876, *Evening Mail*, 5 May 1876, *Tenbury Wells Advertiser*, 16 May 1876, *Penrith Observer*, 14 August 1883, *Leeds Mercury*, 28 April 1887. The miniature by Cosway which depicted Kitty Fisher in the character of a Magdalen was sold by the Hon Felton Hervey, youngest son of the Earl of Bristol, in a sale at Christie's, 1775. The Rupert Barber miniature was owned by Dr Charles and Nathaniel Chauncy who also held a miniature of Kitty by Luke Sullivan. A portrait of 'the charming Kitty Fisher' by Ozias Humphry was included in an exhibition of miniatures at Brussels in 1912. *The Times*, 17 April 1912.

17. The reference to Kitty living at Titsey Place in 1763 comes from the *Surrey Mirror*, 27 September 1884. *Public Advertiser*, 2 July 1765.

18. Matthew Dodd's execution took place on 19 August 1763. *Public Advertiser*, 12 July and 1 August 1763, *Salisbury and Winchester Journal*, 22 August 1763, *Derby Mercury*, 12 August and 26 August 1763, *Leeds Intelligencer*, 30 August 1763. *The Grenville papers, being the correspondence of Richard Grenville, Earl Temple, and the Right Hon George Grenville, their friends and contemporaries*, vol 2 (J. Murray, 1852). The New Gaol has since been demolished; Newington Gardens park now occupies the site.

19. *Gazetteer and London Daily Advertiser*, 28 November 1763. Kitty sat to Reynolds on 20 July 1764.

20. Domenico Negri opened the Pot and Pineapple in 1757. By the end of the century, it was known as Gunter's Tea Shop and became a fashionable Regency

destination. The Land Tax records for 1764 record Kitty as Mrs Cath Fisher at Bruton Street and as Mrs Martin on Carrington Street. Presumably, the move from Carrington to Bruton Street took place during this year. Her parents remained in the Carrington Street house; in 1765, Mrs Martin is crossed out and Jn Henry Fisher is overwritten in the Land Tax record for that street.

21. *London Chronicle*, 23–26 February 1765: 'On Saturday advice was received from the South of France, of the death of the Hon. William Richard Chetwynd, Esq; son and heir to Lord Viscount Chetwynd, and Member for Stafford.' Elizabeth Chetwynd remained a widow until December 1778 when she made a second marriage to Jeffrey Thompson which, oddly, seems to have been celebrated on 16 December at Norwich and 17 December at St Mary le Tower in Ipswich. The viscountcy, which should have been inherited by William, instead passed sideways to his father's younger brother. William's sister, Catherine, the widow of John Talbot, son of Charles Talbot, 1st Baron Talbot, inherited Ingestre Hall and the estate.

22. *Lloyd's Evening Post*, 15–18 Mar 1765 reported that Chetwynd's embalmed body was en route to England. This report stated that he died in Limoges, whereas all earlier reports had given the south of France. Possibly Limoges was a stop on the journey home? It was the naturalist and travel writer Thomas Pennant who recorded the *contretemps* over the body in Paris, in his *Tour on the Continent, 1765* (Ray Society, 1948). His diary entry was dated 5 April 1765.

23. *The Covent Garden Ladies: Pimp General Jack and the Extraordinary Story of Harris's List* (Tempus, 2005) by Hallie Rubenhold. *The Meretriciad* (1761).

24. Lucy Cooper died in October 1772.

25. Nathaniel Hone's portrait of Kitty is now in London's National Portrait Gallery. The Beaney in Canterbury owns another portrait by Nathaniel Hone, in which the sitter is believed to be Kitty Fisher. While there is a distinct resemblance, the eyes of the lady in the portrait appear dark, rather than Kitty's cerulean blue. However, it may be that this portrait was painted after Kitty's death but intended to represent her, or that the colours have darkened through age.

26. The society comprised 211 members in 1765. *Public Advertiser*, 10 May 1765.

27. John Henry Fischer was buried on 26 September 1765. Kitty sat to Reynolds on 28 September. The *Public Ledger*, 21 September 1765, carried an advert for the lease of Titsey Place, noting that it was to be let unfurnished, and it had been 'late in the occupation of W. R. Chetwynd, Esq.' which proves his (and therefore Kitty's) residence at the house in the absence of any lease agreements.

28. David Mannings, who compiled Reynolds's *catalogue raisonné*, thought this portrait to be Reynolds's most erotic, quoted in *Joshua Reynolds: The Life and Times of the First President of the Royal Academy* by Ian McIntyre. This portrait is now in the Gemäldegalerie, Berlin. It was sold at Christie's, 4 May 1810, by Caleb Whitefoord to John Symmons for £2 2s, as a 'sketch of Kitty Fisher as Danaë by Joshua Reynolds'. Symmons in turn sold it (29 March 1828) at Harry Phillips's saleroom in London, as a 'sketch of Kitty Fisher and Child by an anonymous artist'. Getty Provenance Index.

29. Woolf, Maurice. 'Joseph Salvador 1716–1786.' *Transactions (Jewish Historical Society of England)*, vol. 21, 1962, pp. 104–137. Accessed via JSTOR. Woolf says that Salvador's wife, Leonora, had died by 1766.

30. Old Bailey Online (www.oldbaileyonline.org): Charles Johnson, Theft: grand larceny, 11 December 1765. The robbery occurred on 20 November. *The Complete Book of Emigrants in Bondage, 1614–1775* by Peter Wilson Coldham (Genealogical Publishing Company, 1988). Few transportation records from this period survive: before 1776 all transported convicts went to either North America or the West Indies. The Old Bailey session papers list Charles Johnson among the convicts who were 'severally ordered to be transported to some of His Majesty's Colonies and Plantations in America for the space of seven years.' Histories of the Tête-à-Tête annexed: or, Memoirs of Lord M___t and Mrs L__b__d' in *The Town and Country Magazine, or, Universal Repository of Knowledge, Instruction, and Entertainment* for February 1780.

Chapter 7

1. Catherine was the daughter of John Lynch, the Dean of Canterbury Cathedral. Ripple is also known as Ripple Vale. Tythegston Court was remodelled in two phases from 1766 into the late Georgian mansion which stands today. John Norris was Captain of Deal Castle from 1766 to 1774. *Newsletter of the Friends of the National Museum, Cardiff,* November 2011. Henry Knight and Catherine, née Lynch, married at St Anne's in Soho on 27 March 1762. Their three sons were all christened at Christ Church Cathedral in Canterbury: Henry, 7 July 1763, Robert, 3 September 1764 and William Henry on 18 February 1766. It remains a possibility that John Norris had fathered a son in 1764. There is a baptism at Marylebone on 29 October 1764 for John Powlett Norris whose parents are John Norris Esq and Frances. In John Norris's sister's will (NA PROB 11/1658/109, Will of Elizabeth Norris, Spinster of East Malling, Kent), a John Powlett Norris Esq is named, with no relationship given. He had an appointment in the Post Office.

2. John Pollard and Sarah Louisa Fischer married on 22 March 1766 by special licence and with the consent of Sarah's mother, Anne Fischer.

3. *Kitty's Attalantis* (London, 1766). It had certainly been published by 4 April 1766 when the *Public Advertiser* said, 'We hear that a certain Gentleman in the City, by Advice of his Friends, is come to a Resolution to prosecute the Author of a Pamphlet entitled "Kitty's Attalantis," for abusing his Wife in a most shameful Manner.' Anne Fischer probably lived in the parish of St Ann's, Soho until her death. A burial in the chancel vault at St Martin-in-the-Field, Westminster on 22 May 1771 may be hers. The burial fee book from the church records payments for the funeral which covered prayers, candles, black drapes, and the tolling of the great bell.

4. Horace Walpole's letter was dated 1 March 1766. On 6 November 1777, at St George, Hanover Square, Louisa (as Louisa Skrine) married Sir Thomas

Clarges, Baronet. Jane Sumner and William Skrine had married at the same church, 21 May 1764. Jane Skrine's will was written in Rome on 26 December 1765. It was proved in London on 17 September 1766. NA PROB 11/922/146. As Jane directed that her brother should be Louisa's guardian if Skrine married again, the suggestion is that Skrine was Louisa's stepfather, rather than her actual father. William Skrine did make a second marriage, but not until 18 August 1777 (at St Pancras) when he married Marie Julie Dufay (or Siordet), said to be of Piedmont. On 8 March 1783, Skrine suffered a devastating loss playing cards at Brooks's. Unable to face the consequences, he went to a tavern in Newgate Street and shot himself in the head.

5. The sitting took place on 30 September 1766. In *Life and Times of Sir Joshua Reynolds: with notices of some of his contemporaries* by Charles Robert Leslie and Tom Taylor (John Murray, London, 1865), the editor says that, 'In Sir Joshua's notes on his own practice, – "Miss Kitty Fisher: face cerata (i.e. rubbed with wax), drapery painted with wax and afterwards varnished". This refers to the present picture [the 30 September 1766 sitting]: from about this time he began to note his experiments, and, I think, to indulge in more latitude in making them, choosing for this purpose, however, *pictures he did not care much about*, as he told Mr. Cribb, his frame-maker, from whose son I have the information.'

6. The Marriage Act 1753, better known as Lord Hardwicke's Marriage Act, came into force on 25 March 1754. John Norris gave his address as St James's, and Kitty's was St George's, Hanover Square, both in Westminster. Kitty's name was recorded as Catherine Maria Fischer. Bartholomew Bower, precentor of Haddington, was mentioned in a list of Jacobite rebels with the claim that he had 'carried messages & commissions for the rebels & publickly insulted the well affected to the Government' ('List of Persons Concerned in the Rebellion, 1745–1746', *Publications of the Scottish History Society*, vol. VIII, September 1890). It seems that this was the same man who witnessed Kitty's Scottish wedding.

7. *London Evening Post*, 18–20 November 1766. Kitty's second marriage took place on Thursday, 4 December 1766. Sarah Louisa Pollard née Fischer died (in York Street, near the Middlesex Hospital) on 16 December and was buried at St Anne's in Soho on 19 December 1766, almost exactly nine months after her marriage and so it appears likely that her death was due to complications in childbirth. No baptism nor burial for a child has been found, indicating that the child was stillborn and buried, unnamed, with Sarah Louisa. *Gazetteer and New Daily Advertiser*, 19 December 1766.

8. Almost a century later, a woman who remembered hearing tales of Kitty from her mother said that she 'was a good wife, and greatly beloved by the village poor. She was a celebrated horsewoman. She used to accompany her husband in his rides over the estate and neighbourhood. It was well known she allowed no gates to be opened for her, but cleared them with ease and grace. She rode a beautiful high-spirited blood mare, as black as jet' (*Notes and Queries*, 3rd series, volume VIII, August 1865).

9. Information on the Cosway miniature of Kitty from Sotheby's cataloguing notes which were compiled with assistance from Stephen Lloyd. The miniature was included in a sale in 2005; unfortunately, the provenance given for the miniature did not give the original owner. In the early 1900s, it was owned by the collector, Francis Wellesley, then sold at Sotheby's in 1920 and later included in the 1926 Levenhulme sale in New York where it fetched $700. The miniature is signed and dated Cosway/1767. *New York Times*, 1 and 3 March 1926. Sotheby's: www.sothebys.com/en/auctions/ecatalogue/2005/watercolours-portrait-minatures-l05171/lot.223.html. Sotheby's notes mention 'a miniature of Kitty Fisher with a dove is recorded and although traditionally attributed to Ozias Humphrey it may be by Cosway and either after or perhaps the original design for his 1773 print of Miss Woolls.' The provenance for the Cosway is given as: Francis Wellesley, his sale in these Rooms, 28th June–2nd July 1920, lot 111; Owen D. and Josephine Edmonds Young, New York, 1920; Leverhulme Sale, Anderson, New York, 2nd–4th March 1926, lot 89; Laura Rockefeller and James R. Case III, 1956.

10. The claim was made in a letter from A. H. Howard of Burnwood, New York, dated 23 March 1929 and printed in the *New York Times*, 26 March 1929. The letter reads: 'I have in my possession a small pane of old bottle glass, about 4 by 4 inches, on which is scratched very clearly with a diamond "Kitty Fisher, 1767." This was taken from an old bedchamber of the famous old Castle Inn at Marlborough, England, now the more famous Marlborough College. My father, born in 1793, was for twenty years the superintendent or steward of the college, and on finding this glass preserved it. His father, born in 1750, was at one time connected with "Old Drury" and at Kitty's death was about 17 years of age – old enough to have heard many tales of the actress which in later days he no doubt retold "with advantages" to his sons. As is well known, the Castle Inn was the resting place of the great people of that time, on their way to Bath. So this may have been the last time Kitty wrote her name, as she died the same year. The glass has been in the possession of my family for eighty years, and in mine for fifty.'

11. The newer Queen's Bath had been built over a circular Roman bath. The first Pump Room opened in 1706. *Bath Chronicle and Weekly Gazette*, 30 January 1766, 4 December 1766 and 24 September 1767.

12. Richard 'Beau' Nash had died in 1761. Letter from Elizabeth Montagu dated 1740 and printed in *The Edinburgh Review: Or, Critical Journal*, 1810.

13. *St James's Chronicle or the British Evening Post*, 10–12 March 1767. The name Norris is written in pencil against 21 May 1767 in Reynolds's pocketbook, and John Norris is recorded as a sitter on the 23 and 27 of that month.

Chapter 8

1. John Norris senior died 12 November 1767. Kitty's John Norris wrote to Jeremiah Curteis of Rye from Welbeck Street, the letter dated 6 December, but

with no year entered. The letter concerned a nomination for the Commission of the Peace for Kent (East Sussex Record Office, FRE/6698). While there is no year on the letter, it is most probable that it was written in 1767, given what was about to occur. Etheldred Catherine Knight had been born, at Welbeck Street, on 13 August 1767, and privately christened in the Oxford Chapel, otherwise St Peter, Vere Street and sometimes referred to as the Marybone or Marylebone Chapel. She was then publicly baptised at Tythegston in Wales, 3 December 1767. Had John Norris been left the use of the Welbeck Street house while the Knights travelled to their Welsh estate, perhaps even to stay over the Christmas period? John Norris's Hemsted Park was demolished in the mid-1860s and a new house built. It is now a private boarding school for girls, Benenden School. Anne, Princess Royal attended the school.

2. The house on Charles Street was owned by a hatter, Thomas Robson, and Catherine was there in January 1769. She took the house on Ham Common in July 1769.

3. Back at Ham Common, Catherine was once more known as Catherine Knight. There is no mention of her newborn daughter, and it remains unknown whether she was fostered out or was taken to Ham Common. No definite baptism has yet been found but, given that the couple were using Johnson as a surname, there is one at St James's, Piccadilly on 25 November 1769 for a girl named Emma, the daughter of John and Catherine Johnson, born on the same day as Catherine's daughter, 15 November 1769. If this is her, then Catherine went to extreme lengths to hide her daughter's existence from her husband. John Norris's sister's will mentioned a niece called Elizabeth, the wife of a Mr Norman, probably the Rev John Henry Norman of Ulcombe in Kent. NA PROB 11/1658/109, Will of Elizabeth Norris, Spinster of East Malling, Kent.

4. *Trials for Adultery, Or, The History of Divorce* (The Lawbook Exchange, Ltd, 2006). NA: Salvador v Norris b.r. C 12/1035/32, 1770. Woolf, Maurice. 'Joseph Salvador 1716—1786.' *Transactions (Jewish Historical Society of England)*, vol. 21, 1962, pp. 104–137. There is a burial for a three-year-old William Knight on 23 December 1770 at Westminster; this may be Catherine and Henry Knight's youngest son. Around the same time, Henry Knight commissioned a portrait of himself and his children by Johan Zoffany. There are only three children on the portrait, Henry, Robert, and Etheldred Catherine. The portrait was possibly a pointed rebuke to Catherine. Likewise, Henry Knight's will, dated 22 June 1771, does not mention William Henry. It does, however, mention his natural son, Henry Hobbeson, whom he had fathered upon his servant, Anne Hobbes. Henry Knight died in 1772, leaving his eldest children in the care of his aunt, Anne Bassett. Catherine was still denied access to them (NA, PROB 11/977/118, Will of Henry Knight of Tythegston, Glamorganshire). John Norris and Catherine Lynch married at St George's, Hanover Square, on 12 March 1771. She gave her residence as Sunning in Berkshire. The *Kentish Gazette*, 22 December 1781, reported Catherine's death. John Norris mentioned his son in a letter dated 17 October 1804 (NA, HO 42/77/32).

There is a possible baptism for this son, just as John Norris, on 23 April 1772 at St George, Hanover Square (and if so, then his birth date was 20 April 1772).

5. John Norris died on 8 April 1811 (*Kentish Weekly Post*, 19 April 1811). His burial took place ten days later. Information on his Pentonville address from *Benenden Letters* (London, 1901).

Chapter 9

1. Old Bailey Online: Mary Harris, Louise Smith, 10 May 1769. *Gazetteer and New Daily Advertiser*, 10 July 1769, *General Evening Post*, 24–26 April 1770 and *Morning Chronicle*, 13 November 1772.
2. Kitty Clarke's antics were reported in the *St James's Chronicle or the British Evening Post*, 21–23 May 1761.
3. *London Journal*, 17 February 1722.
4. *New York Sings: 400 Years of the Empire State in Song* by Jerry Silverman (State University of New York Press, 2009).
5. *The songs, recitatives, airs, duets, trios, and chorusses, introduced in the pantomime entertainment, of The enchanted castle, as performed at the Theatre-Royal, Covent-Garden. The words by Miles Peter Andrews, Esq; and the music by Mr. Shields*, 1786.

Bibliography

Ackroyd, Peter, *Revolution: The History of England*, vol. IV (Pan Books, 2017)

Amphlett, Hilda, *Hats: A History of Fashion in Headwear* (Courier Corporation, 2012)

Anecdote, Sir Andrew, *A Collection of Interesting Biography. Containing, I. The life of S. Johnson, LL.D. abridged, principally, from Boswell's celebrated memoirs of the Doctor: II. The life of Mr. Elwes (abridged) by Captain Topham: III. The life of Captain Cook (abridged) by Dr. Kippis* (Dublin, 1792)

Arnold, Catherine, *City of Sin: London and its Vices* (Simon & Schuster, 2010)

Barker, Elizabeth E., *Joseph Wright of Derby in Liverpool* (Yale University Press, 2007)

Bleackley, Horace, *Casanova in England, being the account of the visit to London in 1763-4 of Giacomo Casanova, chevalier de Seingalt; his schemes, enterprises & amorous adventures, with a description of the nobility, gentry & fashionable courtesans whom he encountered, as told by himself* (A. A. Knopf, New York, 1925)

Bleackley, Horace, *Ladies Fair and Frail: Sketches of the Demi-monde During the Eighteenth-Century* (London, 1906)

Bleackley, Horace, *The Story of a Beautiful Duchess, Being an Account of the Life and Times of Elizabeth Gunning, Duchess of Hamilton and Argyll* (London, 1907)

Bond, James, *Somerset Parks and Gardens: A Landscape History* (Somerset Books, 1998)

Burney, Frances, *The Diary and Collected Letters of Madame D'Arblay, Frances Burney* (e-artnow, 2018)

Cardwell, John Henry, Freeman, Herbert Bentley and Wilton, George Clement, *The Clergy of St Anne's, Soho, Two Centuries of Soho, its Institutions, Firms and Amusements* (London, 1898)

Casanova de Seingalt, Jacques, *The Memoirs of Casanova, the Rare Unabridged Edition* (London, 1894)

Casanova de Seingalt, Jacques, *The Memoirs of Jacques Casanova de Seingalt, Volume 1: The Venetian Years* (Start Publishing LLC, 2013)

Casanova de Seingalt, Jacques, *Memoirs de Jacques Casanova de Seingalt, écrits par lui-même*, volume 6 (Brussels, J. Rozez, 1871)

Chetwynd-Stapylton, Henry Edward, *The Chetwynds of Ingestre: Being a History of that Family from a Very Early Date* (Longman's, Green and Co., 1892)

Cleland, John, *Memoirs of a Woman of Pleasure* (London, 1748)

Cock-Starkey, Claire, *The Georgian Art of Gambling, Being a Miscellaneous Collection of Fashionable Card Games and Diverse Pastimes* (British Library, 2013)

Coldham, Peter Wilson, *The Complete Book of Emigrants in Bondage, 1614–1775* by Peter Wilson Coldham (Genealogical Publishing Company, 1988)

Conway, Alison Margaret, *Private Interests: Women, Portraiture, and the Visual Culture of the English Novel, 1709–1791* (University of Toronto Press, 2001)

Earle, Alice Morse, *Costume of Colonial Times* (Read Books Ltd, 2013)

Evans, Jennifer and Read, Sara, *Maladies and Medicine: Exploring Health & Healing, 1540–1740* (Pen & Sword Books, 2017)

FitzGerald, Brian (ed.), *Correspondence of Emily, Duchess of Leinster (1731–1814), vol. III: Letters of Lady Louisa Conolly and William, Marquis of Kildare (2nd Duke of Leinster)* (Dublin, 1957)

Gay, John, *The Beggar's Opera* (London, 1728)

Gervat, Claire, *Elizabeth: The Scandalous Life of an 18th Century Duchess* (Random House, 2011)

Gibson, Robin, *The Face in the Corner: Animals in Portraits from the Collection of the National Portrait Gallery* (National Portrait Gallery Publications, 1998)

Greig, James (ed.), *The Diaries of a Duchess: Extracts from the Diaries of the First Duchess of Northumberland (1716–1776)* (Hodder & Stoughton, 1926)

Hardy, Charles Frederick (ed.), *Benenden Letters: London, Country, and Abroad 1753–1821* (London, J. M. Dent & Co., 1901)

Haslewood, Francis, *The Parish of Benenden, Kent: Its Monuments, Vicars, and Persons of Note* (Ipswich, 1889)

Henderson, Tony, *Disorderly Women in Eighteenth-Century London: Prostitution and Control in the Metropolis, 1730–1830* (Taylor & Francis, 2014)

Ireland, John, *Letters and Poems of the Late Mr John Henderson, with Anecdotes of His Life* (London, 1786)

Knight, Charles (ed.), *London, Volume 1* (Charles Knight & Co., 1841)

Leslie, Charles Robert and Taylor, Tom, *Life and Times of Sir Joshua Reynolds* (J. Murray, 1865)

Lewis, W. S and St Brown, Jr., Ralph (eds), *Horace Walpole's Correspondence with George Montagu*, vol. 1 (Yale University Press, 1941)

Linnane, Fergus, *Madams: Bawds and Brothel-Keepers of London* (The History Press, 2001)

Major, Joanne and Murden, Sarah, *A History of the Dukes of Bolton 1600–1815: Love Loyalty* (Pen & Sword Books, 2020)

McCreery, Cindy, *The Satirical Gaze: Prints of Women in Late Eighteenth-century England* (Clarendon Press, 2004)

McIntyre, Ian, *Joshua Reynolds: The Life and Times of the First President of the Royal Academy* (Penguin, 2004)

Montagu, Elizabeth, *Elizabeth Montagu, the Queen of the Blue-Stockings: Her Correspondence from 1720 to 1761 by her Great-great-niece Emily J. Climenson*, vol. II (John Murray, London, 1906)

Namier, Ralph (ed.), *The History of Parliament: The House of Commons, 1754–1790* (Secker & Waring, 1964)

Neal, John Preston and Moule, Thomas, *Views of the Seats of Noblemen and Gentlemen, in England, Wales, Scotland, and Ireland*, vol. 4 (London, 1820)

Nevill, Ralph, *Light Come, Light Go: Gambling, Gamester, Wagers, The Turf* (Macmillan & Co, 1909)

Paulson, Ronald, *Hogarth: Art and Politics, 1750–1764* (James Clarke & Co., 1993)

Peakman, Julie, *Amatory Pleasures: Explorations in Eighteenth-Century Sexual Culture* (Bloomsbury, 2016)

Pennant, Thomas, *Tour on the Continent, 1765* (Ray Society, 1948)

Penny, Nicholas, *Reynolds: Catalogue of a Royal Academy of Arts Exhibition* (Royal Academy of Arts, 1986)

Piozzi, Hester Lynch, *The Piozzi Letters: 1805–1810*, vol. 4 (University of Delaware Press, 1996)

Piozzi, Hester Lynch, *Thraliana: The Diary of Mrs Hester Lynch Thrale (later Mrs Piozzi), 1776–1809*, vol. 1 (1776–1784) (Clarendon Press, 1942)

Pitt, William, *Correspondence of William Pitt, Earl of Chatham*, vol. 2 (John Murray, 1838)

Pyle, Edmund, *Memoirs of a royal chaplain, 1729–1763; the correspondence of Edmund Pyle, D.D. chaplain in ordinary to George II, with Samuel Kerrich D.D., vicar of Dersingham, rector of Wolferton, and rector of West Newton* (John Lane: The Bodley Head, London & New York, 1905)

Rizzo, Betty, *Companions Without Vows: Relationships Among Eighteenth-Century British Women* (University of Georgia Press, 2008)

Robilant, Andrea di, *A Venetian Affair* (Alfred A. Knopf, 2003)

Rosenthal, Laura J., *Infamous Commerce: Prostitution in Eighteenth-Century British Literature and Culture* (Cornell University Press, 2015)

Rubenhold, Hallie, *Harris's List of Covent Garden Ladies: Sex in the City in Georgian Britain* (Tempus, 2005)

Rubenhold, Hallie, *The Covent Garden Ladies: Pimp General Jack and the Extraordinary Story of Harris's List* (Tempus, 2005)

Silverman, Jerry, *New York Sings: 400 Years of the Empire State in Song* (State University of New York Press, 2009)

Smith, John Thomas, *Nollekens and His Times: Comprehending a Life of that Celebrated Sculptor: and Memoirs of Several Contemporary Artists, from the Time of Roubiliac, Hogarth and Reynolds to that of Fuseli, Flaxman and Blake*, vol. 1 (Henry Colburn, 1828)

Smith, William James (ed.), *The Grenville Papers: The Correspondence of Richard Grenville, Earl Temple, K.G. and the Right Hon. George Grenville, their friends and contemporaries*, vol. 1 (John Murray, 1852)

Thornury, Walter, *Old and New London: A Narrative of Its History, Its People, and Its Places* (Cassell, 1887)

Tillyard, Stella, *A Royal Affair: George III and his Troublesome Siblings* (Random House, 2010)

Tillyard, Stella, *Aristocrats: Caroline, Emily, Louisa, and Sarah Lennox, 1740–1832* (Chatto & Windus, 1994)

Tyreman, Christopher, *History of Harrow School, 1324–1991* (Oxford University Press, 2000)

Walpole, Horace, *The Correspondence of Horace Walpole, with George Montagu, Esq., and Others: 1760–1769* (Henry Colburn, 1837)

Wheatley, Henry B., *London Past and Present, a Dictionary of its History, Associations, and Traditions*, vol. 2 (John Murray, 1891)

Woolley, Hannah, *The Gentlewoman's Companion: Or, A Guide to the Female Sex* (London, 1675)

Archival Sources, Libraries, and Galleries

East Sussex Record Office

Ninth Report of the Royal Commission on Historical Manuscripts, Part II (H. M. Stationery Office, 1884)

Catalogue of an Important Sale of Original First Class Oil Paintings being the Entire Collection of Mr. A. D'Huyvetter of Antwerp to be sold at the Leeds Art Galleries, Nos. 817 and 819 Broadway (New York, 1900)

Catalogue of Pictures in the Collection of Beriah Botfield, Esq. at Norton Hall (London, 1848)

Catalogue of Pictures, Drawings and Miniatures, the Property of Lord Hylton (privately printed, 1903)

Harvard Art Museums

Kent Archives

Lewis Walpole Library, Yale University

National Library of Scotland

Staffordshire Record Office

The Beaney, Canterbury Museums

The Goldsmith's Company, Library and Archives

The National Archives (as referenced in the text and endnotes)

The Rijksmuseum, Amsterdam

Trials for Adultery, Or, The History of Divorce (The Lawbook Exchange, Ltd, 2006)

Yale Center for British Art

Periodicals

Bengal Past and Present, vol XXXVII, Part 1, serial no. 73, January–March 1929

Blackwoods Edinburgh Magazine, vol. 15, January–June 1844

The Antiquarian Magazine & Bibliographer, vol. 3, 1883

The Edinburgh Review, or, Critical Journal, 1810

The Gentleman's Magazine, vol. 88, 1800

The Westminster Magazine, February 1773

Town and Country Magazine, or Universal Repository of Knowledge, Instruction, and Entertainment:

Histories of the Tête-à-tête annex'd; or, Memoirs of Honoris and Mrs Wh__te, July 1769

Histories of the Tête-à-tête annex'd: or, Memoirs of the Old Soldier and Hebe W_ts_n, April 1770

Histories of the Tête-à-tête annex'd; or, Memoirs of Ad__l K__], and Mrs W_lls, September 1771

Histories of the Tête-à-tête annex'd: or, Memoirs of the Universal Gallant and the Cyprian Votary, October 1779

Histories of the Tête-à-tête annex'd Histories of the Tête-à-tête annex'd: or Memoirs of Lord M__t and Mrs L__b__d, February 1780

Histories of the Tête-à-tête annex'd: or, Memoirs of Sir J. Hogstie, and Mrs Floyd, October 1780

Contemporary Newspapers
As referenced in the endnotes.

Contemporary Pamphlets and Publications
Anonymous:

A Catalogue of the Rarities to be seen at Don Saltero's Coffee-House in Chelsea (London, 1780)

A Collection of Songs (Dublin, 1769)

An Odd Letter on a Most Interesting Subject to Miss Kitty Fisher by Simon Trusty (London, 1760)

Harris's List of Covent-Garden Ladies, or, New Atlantis for the Year 1761 (London, 1761)

Histoire de la Vie et des Aventures de la duchesse de Kingston (London, 1789)

Horse and Away to St James's Park, Or, a Trip for the Noontide Air: Who Rides Fastest, Miss Kitty Fisher, or her Gay Gallant (Strawberry Hill, 1759)

Kitty's Attalantis (London, 1766)

Miss Kitty F—h-r's Miscellany, with a Dramatic Sermon by Two Methodist Preachers (London, 1760)

The Adventures of the Celebrated Miss Kitty F____r, or, Who will Fish in a Silver Stream with an hundred Pound Bait. A Comic Satire Addressed to the Gentlemen in the Interest of the above Celebrated Miss (London, 1759)

The remonstrance of Harris, pimp-general to the people of England. Setting forth his many schemes in town and country, for the service of the public, and the ungrateful treatment he has met with (London, 1759)

The songs, recitatives, airs, duets, trios, and chorusses, introduced in the pantomime entertainment, of The Enchanted Castle, as performed at the Theatre-Royal, Covent-Garden. The words by Miles Peter Andrews, Esq; and the music by Mr. Shields (London, 1786)

*The Uncommon Adventures of Miss Kitty F****r* (London, 1759)

Trials for Adultery, Or, The History of Divorces. Being Select Trials at Doctors Commons for Adultery, Cruelty, Fornication, Impotence, &c, from the Year 1760, to the Present Time (London, 1779)

A genius (thought to be Samuel Derrick), *Memoirs of the Bedford Coffee-House*, 2nd edition (London, 1763)

Campbell, R., *The London Tradesman, Being a Compendious View of All the Trades, Professions, Arts, Both Liberal and Mechanic, Now Practised in the Cities of London and Westminster. Calculated for the Information of Parents, and Instruction of Youth in Their Choice of Business* (London, 1747)

Funidos, Rigdum (pseudonym), *Kitty's Stream: or, the Noblemen turned Fisher-men, a Comic Satire addressed to the Gentlemen in the Interest of the Celebrated Miss K___y F____r* (London, 1759)

Mozeen, Thomas, *A Collection of Miscellaneous Essays* (London, 1762)

Seymour, Robert, *A Survey of the Cities of London and Westminster, Borough of Southwark, and Parts Adjacent* (London, 1735)

Strype, John, *A Survey of the Cities of London and Westminster* (London, 1720)

Thompson, Edward, *The Court of Cupid* (London, 1770)

Thompson, Edward, *The Courtesan* (London, 1765)

JSTOR Database

Runaway Registers, Haddington (Continued). (1889). Northern Notes & Queries, 3(12)

Woolf, Maurice. 'Joseph Salvador 1716–1786.' *Transactions (Jewish Historical Society of England)*, vol. 21, 1962

Oxford Dictionary of National Biography

Hanham, A. (2005, May 26). Parsons, Anne [Nancy] [married name Anne Maynard, Viscountess Maynard] (c. 1735–1814/15), courtesan and political mistress

Kilburn, M. (2008, January 3). William Henry, Prince, first duke of Gloucester and Edinburgh (1743–1805)

Lane, J. (2004, September 23). Coventry [née Gunning], Maria, countess of Coventry (bap. 1732, d. 1760), figure of scandal

Mackay, R. Keppel, Augustus, Viscount Keppel (1725–1786), naval officer and politician

McCreery, C. (2004, September 23). Fischer [married name Norris], Catherine Maria [known as Kitty Fisher] (1741?–1767), courtesan.

Postle, M. (2015, September 17). Reynolds, Sir Joshua (1723–1792), portrait and history painter and art theorist

Rodger, N. Anson, George, Baron Anson (1697–1762), naval officer and politician

Stevenson, J. (2004, September 23). Nesbitt [née Davis], Mary (1742/3–1825)

Wood, S. (2004, September 23). Ligonier, John [formerly Jean-Louis de Ligonier], Earl Ligonier (1680–1770), army officer

Online Sources

Ancestry (www.ancestry.com)

Early Georgian Portraits Catalogue: Fisher, National Portrait Gallery (www.npg.org.uk/collections/explore/by-publication/kerslake/early-georgian-portraits-catalogue-fisher)

Findmypast (www.findmypast.com)

Historical Portraits Image Library, Philip Mould (www.historicalportraits.com/Gallery.asp)

Horace Walpole's Correspondence, Yale Edition: Lewis Walpole Library (images.library.yale.edu/hwcorrespondence)

Looking, looking away, virtual exhibition with text by Ruth Jones (University of York) (www.york.ac.uk/history-of-art/virtual-exhibition/thegeorgianface/looking.html)

National Trust: The Characters at Croome (www.nationaltrust.org.uk/croome/the-characters-of-croome)

Revealing New Information about the Courtesan, Nelly O'Brien by Joanne Major (www.georgianera.wordpress.com/2018/12/04/revealing-new-information-about-the-courtesan-nelly-obrien)

Survey of London via British History Online (www.british-history.ac.uk/search/series/survey-london)

The Georgians: What They Ate by Regan Walker (www.georgianera.wordpress.com/2015/07/10/the-georgians-what-they-ate)

The Getty Provenance Index (www.getty.edu/research/tools/provenance/search.html)

The Old Bailey Online (www.oldbaileyonline.org)

Academic Publications

Blind Items: Anonymity, Notoriety, and the Making of Eighteenth-Century by Kevin Jordan Bourque, BA, MA. Dissertation presented to the Faculty of the Graduate School of The University of Texas at Austin in Partial Fulfillment of the Requirements for the Degree of Doctor of Philosophy, August 2012

'Enchanting Witchery': Sir Joshua Reynolds's Portrait of Kitty Fisher as Cleopatra by Bradford Mudge (University of Colorado at Denver)

Miss Kitty: 'Two Girls Decorating a Cat by Candlelight' by Joseph Wright, by Stephen Leach (draft) (www.academia.edu/33348558/Miss_Kitty.docx)

Old Masters and Aspirations: The Randlords, Art and South Africa by Michael Stevenson. Thesis presented for the Degree of Doctor of Philosophy in the Department of Art History, University of Cape Town, September 1997

Reynolds and the double-entendre, The Society of Dilettanti portraits by Robin Simon

Some Talk of Alexander: James Harvey D'Egville and the English Ballet 1770–1836 by Keith Cavers. Thesis submitted in fulfilment of the requirements for the degree of Master of Philosophy, University of Surrey, Department of Dance Studies, September 1994

The Face of Fashion: Milliners in Eighteenth-Century Visual Culture by Kimberly Chrisman Campbell (a paper presented as the Mason Lecture at the BSECS Conference, 12 August 2000)

'The Lives of Kitty Fisher' by Marcia Pointon in the *Journal of Eighteenth-Century Studies*, October 2008

Index